A SUSSEX COOK'S CALENDAR

Menus and recipes for each month of the year

PRUNELLA KILBANE

S. B. Publications

Dedication:
For E F-J, a non-foodie whose
encouragement and hard work on this book only
matches her courage in being an errant moth and
eating her way through it. P K

First published in 1995 by S. B. Publications
c/o 19 Grove Road, Seaford, East Sussex BN25 1TP

ISBN 1 85770 087 2

Printed by Island Press Ltd, 01323 490222 UK

A SUSSEX COOK'S CALENDAR

CONTENTS

ABOUT THE AUTHOR

Prunella Kilbane trained at the Cordon Bleu School in London, opened the capital's first takeaway, Casseroles, in 1947 and followed that with a dial and dine delivery service to the boardrooms of the City. Her next project was a country house hotel at Singleton, and a few years later she opened her first restaurant, the Curry Club, in Chichester. In 1965 she moved to Devon and a year later opened the Elbow Room in Totnes. This had seating for 20 opposite a car park for 200, and was an immediate and lasting success. Prince Charles gave a private party there, it received an AA Rosette, and had constantly to expand to cope with its customers, ending up as Even More Elbow Room. Since she retired Prunella, who now lives in Lewes, writes on cookery for magazines, occasionally broadcasts on the subject, and also paints.

Weights and measures

OVEN TEMPERATURE CHART

Centigrade	Fahrenheit	Gas No.	
110	225	$\frac{1}{4}$	Very slow
120	250	$\frac{1}{2}$	Very slow
140	275	1	Slow
150	300	2	Slow
160	325	3	Moderate
180	350	4	Moderate
190	375	5	Moderately hot
200	400	6	Moderately hot
220	425	7	Hot
230	450	8	Hot

METRIC CONVERSION

Exact conversion from Imperial to metric is not convenient for shopping so I am suggesting metric measures rounded off into units of 25, which will normally be slightly less than the Imperial equivalents.

Ounces	Grams	Ounces	Grams
1	25	11	300
2	50	12	350
3	75	13	375
4	100	14	400
5	150	15	425
6	175	16 (1lb)	450
7	200	17	475
8	225	18	500
9	250	19	550
10	275	20	575

LIQUID MEASURES

Pints	Mls	Pints	Mls
$\frac{1}{4}$ pt	150 ml	1 pt	600 ml
$\frac{1}{2}$ pt	300 ml	$1\frac{1}{2}$ pt	900 ml
$\frac{3}{4}$ pt	450 ml	$1\frac{3}{4}$ pt	1000 ml (1 litre)

INTRODUCTION

THIS cook's calendar does not just provide menus for each month, with the relevant recipes. It takes account of the Sussex social season and the fruits of the Sussex earth in their season – and its fish, flesh and fowl.

There are gourmet meals for Goodwood, great picnics to take to Glyndebourne, food for fetes and flower shows, barbecues for the beach and, of course, menus appropriate to the festivals of Christmas, Easter, Midsummer and Michaelmas.

Today the food markets are flooded with exotic and out-of-season fruits and vegetables from countries with different climates. It is possible to have strawberries in December and oysters in July, but does one really want them then?

Local grown, local caught, local reared produce is here to be used and savoured. There is no excuse not to cook lovely fish dishes almost all the year round. You can buy fish straight off the boats by the net houses at Hastings and on the quayside at Newhaven, the harbour at Rye. . . or you can take your choice from the day's catch on the beaches at resorts all along the coast.

It was Izaak Walton, the seventeenth century authority on 'fair angling with rod and line' who first praised the quality of the Chichester lobster, the Selsey cockle, the Amberley trout. They are as good, if not better today.

On the Sussex Downs John Ellman reared the sheep that produced the succulent Southdown mutton, which later formed the base stock of the New Zealand lamb industry. The higglers of the Weald fattened chickens for market and train loads of plump Light Sussex went daily to London. Now the poultry industry is battery farmed and refrigerated but there are still plenty of free range chickens in Sussex fields, farmyards and farm shops.

When it comes to growing good things to eat West Sussex has the soil. Worthing tomatoes are among the most succulent, and inland from Selsey it is just one big market garden. Everywhere, in summer, there are invitations to Pick Your Own, and small tables outside cottages with a choice of home grown vegetables – and a discreet tin for the cash.

So let us pick, purchase and plan a culinary path through the twelve months of the year. I have provided twelve dishes for each month; four first courses, four main dishes and four puddings, with a suggested menu for each. Of course they are all interchangeable. For each of the four summer months I have also provided set picnics and in November some suggestions for winter outdoor eating around the bonfire or while watching the fireworks. All the recipes are for four unless otherwise stated.

Bon appetit.

• •

ACKNOWLEDGEMENTS

Through the years I have been given favourite recipes by kind friends and friends' cooks, who in turn have had them passed on from their mothers, even grandmothers. Some of these I have gratefully used, some I have varied to suit my own taste and some I have never used at all, but they have all been filed. Added to these I have cut out hundreds of recipes from periodicals and journals myself and since these have no provenance I may, quite unintentionally, have borrowed someone else's brainchild, so to any publisher or author from whom I may have inadvertently purloined such material I offer my apologies and thanks.

My thanks also to my editor, Brigid Chapman, for her support and encouragement, to Judy Moore for risking literary and gastronomic indigestion while reading the proofs so meticulously, and to Tizzie Knowles for her illustrations for the cover.

JANUARY
••••••••••

AFTER all the hard work in the kitchen that Christmas demands January is a bit of an anti-climax. It is a time to go back to old favourites that are warming and comforting such as lovely hot soups and interesting casseroles and the wonderful English puddings that were all part of our childhood and cookery heritage.

But when midnight chimes and a New Year begins, there is often a gathering of friends and family. While the celebratory bottles are being drained, a few sandwiches or snacks before bedtime might be a good idea.

Celery sandwiches with walnut butter

SOFTEN butter and spread on the bread. Put about eight or ten walnut halves in the blender until finely chopped. Chop two sticks of celery very finely and mix with the walnut, add a pinch of salt, pepper and cinnamon and fill the sandwiches.

Ham, chicken and curried butter sandwiches

MIX an eggspoonful of curry powder into the softened butter, stir well and add a squeeze of lemon juice and a teaspoonful of apricot jam. Chop a slice of ham and half a chicken breast into tiny dice. Mix with the butter and spread on the bread.

Scrambled egg and smoked salmon sandwiches

SCRAMBLE two eggs and cut up one small slice of smoked salmon into very little pieces, mix together and spread the mixture on the buttered bread.

Savoury fillings

FILL ready made or homemade tartlets with a mixture of shrimps with Hollandaise sauce (bottled Benedicta is excellent) or with **smoked trout pate** for which you will need two smoked trout fillets with the skin removed, one ounce (25g) of softened unsalted butter, a teaspoonful of creamed horseradish, squeeze of lemon juice, salt and black pepper. Flake fish into a bowl and blend with the other ingredients until smooth then fill the tartlets with the mixture.

MENUS OF THE MONTH		
First courses	**Main dishes**	**Puddings**
Haggis	Braised oxtail	Apple Charlotte
Artichoke soup	Steak and kidney	Treacle tart
Parsnip and tomato	pudding	Adam and Eve
soup	Casserole of pork	pudding
Egg mayonnaise	Irish stew	Caribbean trifle

ON January 25 Burns Night is celebrated enthusiastically in Sussex by members of the many flourishing Caledonian societies and Scottish families living far south of their border. Haggis is the oldest of the 'pudding' sausages. It is made by stuffing a sheep's stomach with chopped sheep's offal, adding seasoning and oatmeal. The contemporary version is surprisingly palatable and can be found in most supermarkets, either fresh or tinned. In case you feel like making it yourself here is a recipe:

Haggis

8 ozs (225g) lean minced beef
8 ozs (225g) of lamb's liver
2 medium onions peeled
6 ozs (75g) shredded suet

6ozs (75g) oatmeal
salt and black pepper
good pinch of nutmeg

PUT liver into a pan of cold water, bring to the boil and cook for ten minutes. Remove from the heat, drain, and reserve four tablespoons of the water it was cooked in. Spread the oatmeal onto a baking tray and put in a moderate oven (170°C, gas 4) to brown for about 10 minutes. Meanwhile mince the liver with the onions and transfer to a bowl with the oatmeal, minced beef, suet, reserved liquid, salt, pepper and nutmeg and mix well together. Grease a pudding basin of sufficient size to hold the mixture with some space left over for expansion. Cover top of basin with greaseproof paper tied with string, and cover that with a double thickness of foil. Put the basin into a large saucepan, filled with enough water to come up almost to the top of it. Bring to the boil and cook for three hours, topping up with more water to keep it to a rolling boil. Take care not to let it boil dry. Remove the haggis to a suitable serving dish and keep hot until required.

First courses

'Soup of the evening, beautiful soup. . .' sang the Mock Turtle, and I agree with him one hundred per cent. For convenience I have given a stock cube in every recipe but naturally, if you have the time to make your own stock from poultry carcasses and bones from the butcher, it will improve the quality of the soups.

Artichoke soup

1 lb (450g) Jerusalem artichokes	1 pt (600 mls) chicken stock, or a cube
2 medium onions, peeled and sliced	2 ozs (50g) butter
salt and ground black pepper	1/2 pt (300 mls) double cream
1 pt (600 mls) milk	chopped parsley

PEEL, wash and cut up the artichokes. Put the butter in a pan and saute them with the onions for about 10 minutes, stirring from time to time. Add the milk and stock and cook until the vegetables are soft. Remove them with a little of the liquid and put into a blender and puree. Return to the saucepan, mix well with the liquid left in it, adding a little more stock to your required thickness. Season, add the cream and keep hot until ready to serve. Garnish with parsley.

Parsnip and tomato soup
(serves six)

1 oz (25g) butter	1/2 tsp black pepper
2 onions, peeled and thinly sliced	1/2 tsp dried thyme
1 clove garlic, crushed	1 1/2 pts (900 mls) chicken stock
1 lb parsnips, peeled and chopped	5 fl ozs milk
3 tbs flour	1 bay leaf
1 tsp salt	14 ozs (400g) can of tomatoes

IN a large saucepan melt the butter over a moderate heat and fry the onions, stirring occasionally, for about six minutes until they are soft and translucent. Add garlic and parsnips and continue frying for a further four minutes. Remove pan from heat and sprinkle the flour, salt, pepper and thyme over the cooked vegetables. Gradually add the chicken stock, stirring constantly to avoid lumps, then add the milk, bay leaf and tomatoes with their juice. Return pan to heat and bring to boil, stirring constantly. Reduce heat to low, cover pan and simmer for 40 minutes, until parsnips are very tender. Remove from heat and discard bay leaf. Blend until smooth and pour back into saucepan and cook, stirring occasionally, for two to three minutes until thoroughly heated through.

Egg mayonnaise

4 eggs, boiled for ten minutes
4 lettuce leaves
8 strips anchovies
2 tbs capers

½ pt (300 mls) mayonnaise, home
made or Hellmans
chopped parsley or paprika for garnish

PEEL the eggs and cut lengthways into halves. Put the lettuce on each plate and two egg halves, yolk side up. Cover the eggs liberally with mayonnaise and criss-cross the anchovies on top of them. Divide the capers and scatter them on the eggs. Garnish with parsley or paprika

Main dishes

Braised oxtail

4lb (1.8kg) oxtail
1½ tsp salt
½ tsp black pepper
4 ozs (100g) plain flour
1 tbs dripping or lard
2 carrots
2 turnips

2 sticks celery
2 medium sized onions
1½ pts (850mls) beef stock
1 bay leaf
½ tsp dried thyme
4 sprigs parsley

PRE-HEAT the oven to moderate (180°C, gas 4). Trim the oxtail of any fat and cut into pieces. Season the flour and put it into a plastic bag large enough to hold all the meat. Shake the bag about vigorously until each piece of meat is well covered with flour. Melt the fat in a large saucepan over a high heat, add the meat and stir to ensure all the pieces are coated in the fat. Turn frequently until evenly browned and then transfer to a large flameproof casserole. Put all the vegetables, scraped, peeled and roughly chopped up – and extra fat if necessary – in the saucepan you have been using and cook over a moderate heat, stirring frequently until they have softened. Add the vegetables to the meat in the casserole together with the beef stock, bay leaf, thyme and parsley. Place on a high heat and bring the liquid to the boil then cover the casserole and put it in the centre of a moderate oven (160°C, gas 3) and cook for about four hours, or until the meat is coming away from the bone. If the liquid looks low half way through cooking, top it up. With a large spoon skim off all the fat on the surface. If you have the time let it cool overnight, then the fat will be easier to remove and the dish will be less rich. Taste for seasoning and add more if you feel it needs it. Serve with plenty of mashed potatoes.

Steak and kidney pudding

1 lb (450g) stewing steak
6 ozs (175g) kidney, ox or lamb
1 level tbs flour,
salt and pepper
1 large onion, peeled and chopped.
3 tbs cold water

For the suet crust pastry :
1/2 lb (225g) self raising flour
1/2 level tsp salt
1 level tsp baking powder
1/4 lb shredded beef suet
about 1/4 pt (150 mls) cold water to mix

SIFT flour, salt and baking powder into bowl. Add the suet, stir well together and mix to a soft paste with water. Turn out on floured board, knead until smooth and roll out to about an eighth of an inch in thickness. Use two third of the pastry to line a well buttered one and a half pint pudding basin. Cut the steak and kidney into cubes and put into a plastic bag with the flour, salt and pepper and shake until the meat is all covered in flour. Put it into the basin with the onion and add three tablespoonfuls of water. Make a lid with the remaining pastry and press well together to make a seal. Cover with a double thickness of greaseproof paper or buttered foil. Put into a saucepan with some water and steam steadily for three and a half hours. Add more water as and when necessary. Turn out onto a suitable dish by passing a palette knife round the pudding and loosening it away from the basin. Or serve from the basin round which you have folded a clean table napkin.

Casserole of pork

1 1/2 lbs (675g) cubed pork
4 tbs seasoned plain flour
14 oz tin (400g) chopped tomatoes
1 tbs paprika
1 pt (600 mls) chicken stock, from cube
1 tsp Worcestershire Sauce

1 dsp tomato paste
2 tbs prepared English mustard
1/2 tsp ground turmeric
1/2 pt (150mls) of white wine
1 red and 1 green pepper

TOSS the cubed meat in a plastic bag containing the seasoned flour until each piece is covered, then put it into a casserole with all the other ingredients with the exception of the two peppers. Cut each of these in half and remove the ribs and seeds inside. Place them on a tin under the grill, skin side up, turn the heat up to high and leave them to blister and blacken but not burn. Remove, put on a chopping board and take off the skins. Chop the peppers into chunks and add to the casserole. Stir well, pour in hot stock and Worcestershire Sauce and cover. Cook in the oven at 170°C, gas 4 for two hours. Check half way through and stir. If it is on the dry side, add some more wine or stock.

Irish stew

2½ lbs (1.2kg) neck of lamb	1 large peeled and chopped onion
2 level tbs flour	2 level tbs pearl barley
salt and pepper	3 carrots, scraped and chopped
2oz (50g) butter	¾ pt (450 mls) lamb stock, or a cube

DIVIDE the lamb into neat pieces, cutting away the surplus fat. Toss in seasoned flour and fry briskly in a saucepan with hot butter, turning continuously, until brown. Transfer to a plate. Add the onion and carrots to the butter in the pan and fry slowly until pale gold. Now put the meat and vegetables with the pearl barley and the stock into a casserole, cover and place in a moderate oven (170°C, gas 4) and simmer gently for two hours, or until the meat is tender.

Puddings

Apple Charlotte

2 lbs (900g) cooking apples	4 ozs (100g) butter, melted
4 ozs (100g) brown sugar	half a small white loaf, sliced
finely grated rind of 1 lemon	and crusts removed

PEEL, core and slice the apples, put in a pan with sugar and one tablespoonful of water and cook until tender. Add lemon rind and sweeten to taste. Grease a serving dish. Dip sufficient bread in the melted butter to line the dish. Put the apple on top of the bread lining. Cut enough bread into strips to cover the top with each piece overlapping, and dip them into the butter and place on the apple. Put the pie dish on a baking sheet and cook in a medium oven for about 30 minutes, or until the top is crisp.

Treacle tart

1 lb (450g) shortcrust pastry	juice and grated rind of half an
3 ozs (75g) fresh white breadcrumbs	orange or lemon
5 generous tbs golden syrup	1 egg, beaten

PRE-HEAT oven to 200°C, gas 6. Gently heat syrup and stir in breadcrumbs and put on one side to cool. Roll out pastry and with it line a nine inch flan tin, saving all the trimmings. Stir juice and rind into the syrup mixture, place on the base of the pastry case. Re-roll pastry trimmings and cut into narrow strips. Place these criss-cross on the top to create a lattice effect. Brush inside edge of flan with beaten egg. Place in oven on a metal tray, and cook for about 30 minutes or until golden.

Adam and Eve
pudding

1lb (450g) cooking apples, peeled,
cored and thinly sliced
5 ozs (150g) sugar
1 clove

2 tbs cinnamon
4 ozs (100g) butter, softened
4 ozs (100g) self-raising flour
2 eggs, lightly beaten

PRE-HEAT oven to moderate (180°C, gas 4). Put apple slices into medium sized, ovenproof serving dish and sprinkle with cinnamon, add water, clove and 1 oz sugar. Put the butter and remaining sugar into a mixing bowl and beat with a wooden spoon until light and creamy. Add the beaten eggs, a little at a time, beating well between each addition. Sift the flour into the bowl and lightly stir in until no flour particles are visible. Pour the sponge mixture over the apples and spread it evenly with a palette knife. Bake in the middle of the oven for 30 minutes, or until the sponge has risen and begun to turn pale golden brown. Reduce heat to 150°C (gas 2) and continue to cook for a further 30 minutes. Serve immediately with cream.

Caribbean trifle

8 tbs strong black coffee
1 tbs dark rum
4 square trifle sponges, halved
9 ozs (250g) Mascarpone cheese
or cream cheese

1 large banana, peeled and sliced
1 oz (25g) pecan nuts, chopped
7 fl ozs creme fraiche
2 tbs soft brown sugar
pinch ground cinnamon

MIX coffee and rum together. Break up four sponge halves in the base of a glass bowl or dish and pour half the coffee/rum mixture over them and press well down to soak them thoroughly. Mash the banana with the Mascarpone, mix in the nuts and spread over the trifle sponges. Mash remaining four sponge halves with the remaining coffee mixture and spread evenly over the top. Cover with creme fraiche and sprinkle with brown sugar. Chill for two to three hours. Just before serving place under a pre-heated high grill until sugar caramelises. Sprinkle with cinnamon and serve immediately.

● ●

WINTER WARMERS

THERE is nothing like a hot drink on a cold day. A glass or two of punch, mulled wine or spiced ale can speed the parting guest or welcome the arriving one. Alcohol will evaporate if it is overheated so do not bring to the boil.

Pekinese punch

1 bottle red wine	*2 ozs (50g) brown sugar*
1 bottle Dubonnet	*1 tsp cinnamon*
1 pt (600 mls) freshly made China tea	*pinch of nutmeg*
rind and juice of half an orange	*3 cloves*
rind and juice of half a lemon	*orange and lemon slices for garnish*

SIMMER the strained tea in a saucepan with the sugar, fruit rinds and juices, and the spices for 15 minutes. Strain into another saucepan, add the red wine and Dubonnet, and heat quickly, without boiling. Serve in a warm punchbowl with the orange and lemon slices floating on the top.

Mulled Madeira

1 bottle Madeira	*pinch of cinnamon*
2 tbs brandy	*1 oz (25g) sugar*
pinch of ginger	

PUT the ingredients into a pan and simmer gently for a few minutes.

Spiced ale

1 pt (600 mls) mild draught ale	*2 ozs (50g) brown sugar*
2 tbs brandy	*pinch of nutmeg*
twist of lemon peel	

PUT all the ingredients, except the brandy, into a saucepan over a low heat. Remove just as it starts to simmer. Add the brandy and serve.

Grange coffee punch

½ pt (300 mls) red wine	*stick of cinnamon*
2 tbs rum	*grated rind of 2 oranges*
2 pts (1.2 ls) strong black coffee	*8 lumps of sugar*

PUT the grated rind and sugar in a saucepan and pour in the red wine. Let sugar soak up the wine, then add rum and cinnamon stick. Heat gently over a low heat, stirring constantly. Add hot coffee and serve at once.

F̶EBRUARY
············

THE weather can do odd things this month. On February 2 1895 a cricket match was played on the ice covering the lakes at Sheffield Park. In 1960 Lewes station had to be closed because of the flooding but in February the following year there was an unseasonable heatwave and they were sunbathing on the beach at Eastbourne.

Shrove Tuesday is usually in February and that means pancakes. They need not necessarily be the traditional ones, coated with sugar and a generous squeeze of lemon. With various savoury fillings they make a light and tasty main course.

MENUS OF THE MONTH

First courses	Main dishes	Puddings
Pears aux fromage	Boiled mutton with	Bread and butter
Egg and cheese	caper sauce	pudding
mousse	Fillets of sole	Baked bananas
Salmon pate	bonne femme	Steamed coffee
Spinach flan	Braised ribs of beef	pudding
	Savoury pancakes	Oranges in caramel

First courses

Pears aux fromage

2 thick slices bread cut into dice
2 ripe dessert pears, peeled,
cored and sliced
l bunch watercress, washed,
dried and de-stalked
2 tbs butter

4 ozs (100g) crumbled Stilton
or strong Cheddar
4 tbs double cream
freshly ground black pepper
chopped parsley to garnish.

FRY the bread cubes in the butter until crisp to make croutons, then distribute them equally between four ramekin dishes. Put the watercress on top of the croutons and the slices of pears on top of the cress and cover with the crumbled cheese. Spoon the cream over the cheese, a grinding of black pepper on top, and finely chopped parsley to garnish.

Egg and cheese mousse

4 ozs (100g) Roquefort or
Gorgonzola cheese
6 hard boiled eggs, sliced
half a cucumber, peeled,
grated and drained
3 tbs chopped parsley
1 tsp finely chopped onion
1 packet powdered gelatine

¼ pt (150 mls) very hot water
3 tbs lemon juice
½ pt (300 mls) double cream, whipped
salt and pepper
¼ pt (150 mls) of aspic jelly
half a canned pimento, drained
and chopped
tomato and stuffed olives to finsh

MIX together the cheese, cucumber, parsley, pimento and onion. Dissolve the gelatine in a quarter pint of very hot water and add lemon juice and mix well. Cool, then pour into the cheese mixture. Fold in cream and season. Place a well oiled jar in the centre of a souffle dish. When the mixture is on the point of setting spoon a layer into the dish. Cover with a layer of egg slices and repeat the layers until the dish is three quarters full, ending with a layer of mousse. Chill. Meanwhile, make up the aspic jelly according to packet instructions and cool before spooning over the mousse. Allow to set. When the mousse is set run a warm knife round the jar and remove it. Fill the centre with tomato and stuffed olives.

Salmon pate

1 lb (450g) of cooked fresh salmon,
or a large tin of pink or red
4 inch-thick slices white bread.
½ pt (300 mls) milk.
1 oz (25g) soft butter,

1 egg yolk
2 tsp chopped parsley
juice of half a lemon.
salt and pepper.

IF you are using canned salmon, be sure to remove bones and skin, then drain it and flake into a bowl. Remove crusts from bread and soak in the milk until soft. Add the fish and mix up well together. Add the butter, egg yolk, parsley, lemon juice and seasoning. Beat together until well mixed or put into the blender for a few seconds. Turn the mixture into a greased ovenproof dish and cover with foil. Put a roasting pan in the oven with hot water half way up it and put in the fish dish. Cook for one and a quarter hours at 170°C (gas 3). Leave to get cold and then refrigerate. When ready to serve, garnish with chopped parsley and a couple of lemon slices. Hand round hot toast and have butter on the table.

Spinach flan

Short crust pastry
8 ozs (225g) frozen spinach
2 eggs, lightly beaten
2 ozs (50g) butter
2 ozs (50g) cottage cheese

2 ozs (50g) Philadelphia cream cheese
2 ozs (50g) grated Parmesan
5 fl ozs double cream
pinch of mace

THAW the spinach in a colander over a bowl and be sure all the water is out. Roll out the pastry and use it to line a greased eight inch flan dish, a china one if possible so it can come to the table. Melt the butter in a pan and toss the spinach in it. Season with salt and pepper. Mix the cheeses together. Beat the eggs and mix with the cream and mace, add to the cheese and fold in the spinach. Fill the pastry case with the mixture and bake in a pre-heated moderate oven (180°C, gas 4) for half an hour or until the pastry is well done and the flan brown on top.

Main dishes

Boiled mutton with
caper sauce

3lb (1.4kg) leg of lamb
level tsp of salt
2 medium onions, peeled and sliced

2 large carrots, scraped and sliced
4 ozs (100g) diced swede
4 ozs (100g) diced turnip

PUT the lamb into a large saucepan and cover with cold water. Bring slowly to the boil and then remove the scum. Add salt and vegetables, lower the heat and cover pan. Simmer, allowing 25 minutes a pound and 25 minutes over, until it is cooked through and is tender. Test with sharp knife, it may need a little longer. When ready transfer to the centre of a warmed dish containing the vegetables and keep in the oven. This should be served with caper sauce (see recipe on page 92).

> **PASTRY TIP:** If you are using an earthenware flan dish for pastry put it on a metal baking sheet which has been warmed while pre-heating the oven. This will cook the underside of the pastry more quickly.

Fillets of sole
bonne femme

2 Dover sole fillets per person	¼ pt (150 mls) white wine
2 oz (50g) button mushrooms	1 tbs grated strong Cheddar
1 shallot	or Parmesan cheese
1 oz (20g) butter	¼ pt (150 mls) double cream
salt and black pepper	½ pt (300 mls) Bechamel sauce
1 level tbs chopped fresh parsley	mashed potatoes to serve with dish

SKIN the fillets on both sides, wash and dry thoroughly on kitchen paper. Wash and slice the mushrooms and chop the shallot finely. Melt butter and fry shallot until transparent, then add the mushrooms, stir round and cook for a few minutes before adding the parsley and the wine and seasoning with salt and pepper. Poach the fish gently in the pan in this mixture until the fillets are cooked. Remove them to a dish and keep warm. Make the Bechamel sauce (see recipe on page 92) and add to it the ingredients from the pan. Stir well and add the cream. When the sauce is hot, but not boiling, pour it over the fish, sprinkle the cheese over the top and place under a hot grill until golden brown.

Braised ribs
of beef

1½ lbs (675g) lean ribs of beef, cut	large clove of garlic, crushed
into 1½ inch pieces	½ tsp dried marjoram
2 medium sized onions, peeled	4 fl oz beef stock
and coarse cut	1 bay leaf
3 medium carrots, scraped and sliced	

TOSS the cubes of beef in the seasoned flour and fry briskly in hot butter until well brown, turning all the time. Remove to a plate. Add the vegetables to the remaining butter in the pan and fry until pale golden. This will take about seven minutes. Put the vegetables into a flameproof casserole dish and place the meat on top of them. Pour in the beef stock. Bring slowly to the boil, lower the heat and cover the pan. Put the casserole into a moderate oven (180°C gas 4) and cook for about three to three and a half hours, or until the meat is tender.

Savoury pancakes
(Basic batter)

4 ozs (100g) flour
large pinch of salt
1 large egg

1 egg yolk
½ pt (300 mls) milk
1 tbs butter, melted

SIFT flour and salt into a bowl and mix well. Add unbeaten eggs and half the milk. Beat well to a smooth creamy batter. Add the melted butter and then stir in the remaining milk. Beat again thoroughly and leave to rest for about half an hour. When required, heat half an ounce of butter in a frying pan (the larger the pan the thinner the pancake) and pour in two tablespoonfuls of batter. Cook gently on one side until beginning to bubble and firm enough to turn, or toss, and on the other side until firm, without being leathery. Remove from pan and place on greaseproof paper. Continue this method until all the batter is used. The pancakes can be stored overnight in the fridge if desired or filled and served while still hot. Fill them with mixture of your own choice, roll them up and transfer them to an ovenproof dish and cover with a cheese, or other creamy sauce. Bake the pancakes in moderate oven (160°C, gas 3) for approximately 20 minutes, or until sauce is beginning to brown.

Puddings

Bread and butter pudding

6 thin slices of white bread
2ozs (50g) butter
1oz (25g) currants
1oz (25g) sultanas

1½ ozs (40g) castor sugar
2 eggs
1pt (600 mls) milk

REMOVE crusts from bread and spread bread thickly with butter, then cut into fingers or squares and arrange in a two pint buttered heatproof dish. Cover with all the fruit and half of the sugar and top with the remaining bread, buttered sides up. Sprinkle with the rest of the sugar. Beat the eggs and milk well together and pour over the bread in the dish. Leave to stand for half an hour and then bake in the centre of a moderate oven (170°C, gas 4) for an hour, or until the the top is crisp and golden.

FRYING TIP: If you use equal quantities of butter and oil together when frying, the butter will not blacken.

Baked bananas

6-8 bananas
juice from 1 orange
juice from 1 lemon

1 oz (25g) butter
1 tbs castor sugar

PEEL and halve the bananas lengthwise and put them in a buttered oven-proof dish. Mix the sugar with the orange and lemon juice and then pour it over the bananas. Dot all over with the remaining butter and bake in a moderate oven (170°C, gas 4) for 20 minutes.

Steamed coffee pudding

4 egg yolks
2 egg whites
2 ozs (50g) sugar
2 ozs (50g) drinking chocolate powder
¾ pt (450 mls) milk
¼ pt very strong coffee

2 ozs (50g) chopped glace cherries
2 ozs (50g) chopped nuts (optional)
1 oz (25g) crystallised peel,
finely chopped
2 tbs sherry
2 ozs (50g) sultanas

BEAT the eggs in a mixing bowl, add the sugar and chocolate powder and mix well together. Pour over the coffee and the milk, stir and add the rest of the ingredients. Put the mixture into a greased pudding basin, cover with well buttered greaseproof paper or foil and steam gently, without boiling, for about two and a half hours or bake for the same amount of time in a slow oven, (140°C, gas 1) with the basin standing in a dish of warm water. Serve hot or cold. If the latter decorate with curls of chocolate and a little cream.

Oranges in caramel

4 large oranges, peeled,
de-pithed and sliced
juice from half a lemon

For the caramel:
3 tbs water
3 heaped tbs castor sugar

PLACE the orange slices and their juice in a glass serving bowl and pour over the lemon juice. To make the caramel, dissolve the sugar in the water in a pan over a low heat and then increase heat and cook until it turns golden brown. Pour over the fruit and chill until caramel has set.

• •

M<small>ARCH</small>
······

ALTHOUGH the winds can still be cold this is the month the clocks are altered to British Summer Time and the days get longer. There is plenty of good white fish around such as cod, plaice, whiting and haddock, and different vegetables are appearing in the shops. Leeks are usually good at this time of the year, and red cabbages which go so well with a variety of casseroles. Winkles are now in season. There was a time when they were gathered by the ton from the rocks around the coast but now only a few Sussex people eat them. The French, however, call them Escargot le Mer or Escargot a la Rockes and regard them as a delicacy.

MENUS OF THE MONTH

First courses	Main dishes	Puddings
Kipper pate	Guinea fowl casserole	Apple fritters
Avocado cocktail	Baked lamb with	Queen of
Salmon mousse	coriander	puddings
Sardine stuffed	Halibut Hollandaise	Rhubarb fool
eggs	Pork and kidney	Creme brulee
	bean casserole	

First courses

Kipper pate

12 ozs (350g) boned kipper fillets
10 ozs (275g) butter, melted
4 tbs double cream

1 tsp Worcestershire Sauce
1 tbs sherry
black pepper

PUT the kipper fillets in a bowl and pour in enough boiling water to cover them. Leave for ten minutes then pour away water, dry the fillets with kitchen paper, remove the skin and flake the fish. Put into the blender with all the other ingredients and blend until smooth. Spoon into a serving dish. Melt the remaining butter and pour over the pate. Put in the fridge until set. Garnish with parsley.

Avocado cocktail

2 ripe avocados, peeled, stoned and sliced
1 dsp chopped parsley
2 tbs tomato ketchup
½ tsp finely chopped spring onion
1 tsp creamed horseradish

1 tbs olive oil
½ tsp made English mustard
1 tsp lemon juice
salt and black pepper
hard boiled egg for garnish

MARINATE the avocado slices in the seasoned olive oil, the cider vinegar, mustard and lemon juice for half an hour. Mix the remainder of the ingredients together and add them to the avocado slices in the marinade. Serve in individual glasses or dishes and garnish with a little chopped hard boiled egg.

Salmon mousse

Two 7½ oz (214g) cans of salmon
½ pt (300 mls) milk
1 oz (25g) butter
3 tbs flour
2 eggs, separated
¼ pt (150 mls) double cream, whipped
2 tbs tomato ketchup

1 tsp anchovy essence
1 tsp lemon juice
salt and white pepper
4 tsp powdered gelatine
4 tsp boiling water
slices cucumber to garnish

DRAIN the juice from the salmon and put on one side. Remove any skin and bones from the fish and mash the flesh until smooth. Melt the butter, stir in the flour and cook for two or three minutes. Remove from heat and gradually stir in the salmon juice and milk. Bring to the boil and continue to stir until sauce thickens. Remove from the heat and add the egg yolks, allow the sauce to cool slightly and stir in the cream, the tomato ketchup, anchovy essence, lemon juice and seasoning to taste and add to the salmon. Dissolve the gelatine in the boiling water in a small basin. Whisk briskly until it has melted then stir it into the salmon mixture. Whisk the egg whites stiffly and fold these into the mixture. Pour it into a seven inch souffle dish and put in the fridge to set. When ready to serve garnish with slices of cucumber.

> **SAUCE TIP:** If a sauce should curdle or become lumpy put it into the liqidiser and blend until it is smooth.

Sardine stuffed eggs

4 eggs, hard boiled for 10 minutes and
then put into cold water
6 ozs (175g) tin sardines in oil
1 tbs lemon juice

4 tbs mayonnaise, home-made
or Hellmans
1 tbs freshly chopped parsley
salt and white pepper

PEEL the eggs, cut in half and take a slice off the bottom of each half so
they sit flat. Remove the yolks and put into a mixing bowl and mash up
with a fork. Bone and tail the sardines, mash up with the fork, and add
to the egg yolks. Add the remainder of the ingredients and mash everything up again. Fill the whites with the mixture and garnish with parsley. Serve with brown bread and butter.

Main dishes

Guinea fowl casserole

1 guinea fowl
2 tbs oil
1 onion peeled and chopped
2 cloves garlic, peeled and crushed
Salt and black pepper

½ pt (300 mls) chicken stock
¼ pt (150 mls) white wine
4 carrots, peeled and sliced
4 sticks celery cut into inch pieces
2 parsnips, peeled and chopped

HEAT oil in oven proof casserole, put in the bird and cook over a moderate heat, turning it occasionally, until it is nicely browned. Pour in the
stock and wine and bring to the boil then place in a moderate oven
(180°C, gas 4) with the lid on. Cook for 45 minutes then add the vegetables. Season and return to the oven until the bird and the vegetables are
tender. Remove to a serving dish and pour over the cooking juices.

Baked lamb with coriander

half a leg, fillet end, or shoulder of lamb
1 heaped tbs coriander seeds, crushed
2 cloves garlic, sliced lengthways

dripping
small glass white wine

PRE-HEAT the oven to 190°C (gas 5). With a sharp knife make eight
evenly placed incisions in meat and insert slivers of garlic and crushed
coriander. Put meat in roasting tin with knob of dripping and cook in the
oven for 30 minutes per pound. When done transfer to warm serving
dish. Pour off the fat from roasting pan, add the wine to the pan juices
and stir over a low heat, taking care not to let it boil. Pour into a warm
gravy boat. Serve with redcurrant jelly and/or mint sauce or mint jelly.

Halibut Hollandaise

4 large fillets halibut
2½ fl ozs white wine
1 bay leaf
1 slice of onion
8 ozs (225g) crab meat, fresh, frozen or
tinned
2 tbs double cream
½ oz (12g) butter

½ oz (12g) flour
2 egg yolks
4 ozs (100g) melted butter
1 tbs lemon juice
salt and pepper
Hollandaise sauce, home-made or
Benedicta

POACH the fish in a baking dish with the bay leaf, onion slice, wine and just enough water to cover. Put a lid on the dish and cook for approximately 10 minutes in a medium oven. Remove the fish from the baking dish, cover and keep warm. Melt the butter in a saucepan, add the flour, stirring well. Strain in the cooking liquid from the fish, stir well and bring to the boil. Add the cream and bring back to the boil for two to three minutes. Remove from heat, season to taste and mix in crab meat. Put this mixture on the bottom of an ovenproof dish and place the fish on top of it. Keep hot and when ready to serve pour over heated Hollandaise sauce (see recipe on page 91).

Pork and kidney
bean casserole

1 lb shoulder pork, diced into cubes
1 tbs seasoned flour
1 tbs sunflower oil
1 onion, peeled and sliced
3 carrots, scraped and sliced
1 green pepper, de-seeded and sliced

½ pt (300mls) chicken stock made
from a cube
salt and freshly ground black pepper
7½ ozs (212g) can red kidney beans,
drained

TOSS the pork cubes in the seasoned flour. Heat the oil in a frying pan and brown the meat lightly. Remove, drain on kitchen paper if necessary and put in a large ovenproof casserole dish. Saute the carrots, onions and green pepper in a frying pan for about a minute, then add them to the meat in the casserole. Pour in the stock, season lightly with salt and black pepper, cover the casserole with the lid and cook in the centre of a moderate oven (170°C, gas 3) for two hours. Add the kidney beans after approximately one and a half hours.

Puddings

Apple fritters

3 medium cooking apples, peeled,
cored and cut into ¼ inch rings
fat or oil for deep frying
sifted icing sugar for coating
For the batter:

2 ozs (50g) flour
pinch salt
1 level tsp sifted icing sugar
4 tbs warm water
1 dsp unsalted butter, melted

SIFT flour and salt into a bowl. Add sugar and gradually mix to a smooth batter with the water and butter. Whisk the egg white until stiff and fold into the mixture. Coat the apple rings with the batter and fry in the deep hot fat or oil for two to three minutes. Remove from pan and drain on kitchen paper. Dredge thickly with sifted icing sugar. Serve with cream or plain yoghurt.

Queen of puddings

3 ozs (75g) fresh breadcrumbs
1 oz (25g) castor sugar
1 level tsp finely grated lemon peel
¾ pt (450 mls) cold milk
1 oz (25) unsalted butter
yolks of 2 eggs

1 level tbs warmed raspberry jam
For the meringue topping:
2 egg whites
3 ozs (75g) castor sugar
1 level tbs granulated sugar

PUT breadcrumbs, sugar and lemon peel into a basin and mix lightly together. Pour milk into pan, add butter and heat until melted, then pour on to the breadcrumb mixture. Stir well and allow to stand for half an hour. Beat in egg yolks. Spread the mixture into a one and a half pint heatproof dish and bake in the centre of a moderate oven (170°C, gas 4) for about half an hour or until firm and set. Remove from the oven, spread the top with the warmed jam and cover with the meringue.

To make the meringue topping: Put the egg whites into a clean, dry bowl and beat until so stiff that when the bowl is turned upside down they remain where they are. Gently fold in the castor sugar with a large metal spoon and distribute the topping over the pudding and sprinkle over it the granulated sugar. Place in the centre of a moderate oven (180°C, gas 4) for about 10 minutes until meringue is golden brown.

Rhubarb fool

¼ pt (150 mls) custard, home-made or
tinned
12 ozs (350g) rhubarb
4 tbs orange juice

grated rind of half an orange
2 ozs (50g) sugar
pink or red food colouring
2 tbs double cream

MAKE the custard (or open the tin) and cool until lukewarm. Slice the rhubarb, put in a saucepan and cook over a low heat with the orange juice, rind and sugar until well reduced and with a little liquid remaining. Cool and puree with the custard in a blender, or sieve the rhubarb and mix with the custard. Add sufficient colouring to tint to an attractive pink. Pour into individual bowls or glasses and chill. When ready to serve pour on the cream and feather with the handle of a teaspoon.

Creme brulee

yolks of 4 eggs
½ pt (300mls) double cream
3 level tbs sifted icing sugar

l tsp vanilla essence
castor sugar

BEAT the eggs thoroughly. Heat the cream in a double saucepan. Do not allow it to boil. Pour the hot cream onto the egg yolks, beating all the time. Return the mixture to a basin and add the icing sugar and vanilla. Cook without boiling, stirring continuously, until the mixture thickens enough to coat the back of a spoon. Remove from heat and pour into a one pint buttered baking dish or individual ramekins and chill overnight in the fridge. About one hour before serving, sprinkle a quarter inch thick layer of castor sugar over the top of the cream in the dish or ramekins and put under a red hot grill until the sugar caramelises. Chill again until ready to serve. The creme can be accompanied by stewed or fresh fruit in season.

A PRIL

GOODWOOD'S first race meeting was held in hail, wind and rain on the last three days of April in 1802. Now, more weather-wisely, the main meeting is in the summer. And at Horsham long ago they combined the selling of yearling sheep at the spring teg fair with the macabre attractions of public executions. It came to be known as the Hang Fair.

On the food front the new season lamb is here and young carrots, broccoli, good cauliflowers, spring onions. . .

MENUS OF THE MONTH

First courses	Main dishes	Puddings
Quick skillet quiche	Pork chops with	Royal Sussex Delight
Mushroom	peaches	Apple meringue tart
vol au vents	Baked fish with capers	with Calvados
Curried eggs	Braised shoulder	Lemon posset
Smoked haddock	of lamb	Pineapple rice
soup	Sole Veronique	pudding

First courses

Quick skillet quiche

6 ozs (175g) shortcrust pastry
3 eggs
½ pt (300 mls) single cream

6 ozs (175g) grated cheese
salt and ground black pepper
2 large tomatoes, sliced

ROLL out pastry fairly thinly and cut into about a 10 inch circle, using a dinner plate as a guide. Line a non-stick omelette pan with the pastry, pressing it up the sides. Prick all over. Put the pan over a gentle heat and cook for three to four minutes. Beat the eggs with the cream and two thirds of the cheese, and the salt and pepper. Pour into the pastry case, cover and cook for a further three to four minutes. Uncover the pan and top the quiche with sliced tomatoes and sprinkle with the remaining cheese. Put under a pre-heated hot grill until puffed and golden. Slide the quiche onto a plate and serve while hot.

Mushroom vol au vents

4 ready-made vol au vent cases
2 ozs (50g) butter
1½ ozs (40g) flour
½ pt (300 mls) chicken stock or cube
8 ozs (225g) flat mushrooms

1 onion, peeled and finely chopped
2 tbs double cream
chopped parsley for garnish
salt and pepper

PUT the vol-au-vent cases on a baking tray, brush the tops with a little milk and bake in a hot oven (220°C, gas 7) for 20 minutes until crisp and golden. Peel mushrooms and chop half finely and half roughly. Melt butter in pan, add roughly chopped mushrooms and cook for three minutes. Remove with draining spoon and set aside. Add onion to the pan and after one minute the finely chopped mushrooms. Cook for four minutes. Stir in the flour and cook for a further one minute. Remove from heat and gradually stir in the chicken stock. Return to heat and bring to the boil, stirring continuously. Add the cream, rough chopped mushrooms, salt and pepper and simmer for one minute. Fill the vol au vents cases with the hot mushroom filling and keep warm until ready to serve.

Curried eggs

4 hard-boiled eggs, peeled
¾ pt milk
1 tbs medium curry powder
2½ tbs flour
8 ozs (225g) long grain rice, cooked

2 tbs double cream
3 ozs (75g) butter
juice from quarter of a lemon
1 tbs apricot jam
salt and pepper

MELT butter in pan over a low heat and add the flour and curry powder, stir well and blend in the milk. When smooth, add jam and lemon juice. Season well and add the cream. Stir briefly, but do not boil. Transfer to a bowl and allow to cool. To serve arrange the rice in a ring on a serving dish, settle the eggs in the centre of the ring and pour over the sauce.

Smoked haddock soup

1 large smoked haddock
1 large onion, finely diced
4 large potatoes, cooked and
broken up into pieces

1 tbs butter
1 pt (600 mls) milk
salt
6 grindings of black pepper

COOK onion in butter until soft, add the potatoes, mix well and cook together for a further five minutes. Place haddock in a meat pan, pour over milk and cover with kitchen foil. Bake in moderate oven (170°C, gas 4) for about 20 minutes, until flesh comes away from the bone. Allow to cool and then remove the skin and all bones and place fish in a bowl. Strain the milk in which the fish has been cooked into a food processor and add the onions, potatoes and fish. Blend thoroughly. Add seasoning and more milk if a thinner consistency is required. Re-heat to serve and garnish with chopped parsley.

Main dishes

Pork chops with peaches

4 loin pork chops
sunflower oil
4 canned peach halves, drained

4 glace cherries
demerara sugar
watercress for garnish

BRUSH the chops with a little oil and then place them under a pre-heated medium grill for six to 10 minutes, according to thickness. Turn them and brush the other side with oil and grill for a further six to 10 minutes. Two minutes before the end of cooking time, place a peach half on each chop – cut side uppermost. Put a cherry in the centre of each peach half and sprinkle lightly with sugar. Return to the grill and continue cooking to finish the chops, heat the peach and melt the sugar. Garnish with watercress.

Baked fish with soured cream and capers

4 fish steaks, cod, turbot or halibut
2 fl ozs white wine or cider
1½ ozs (40g) butter
½ tsp dried tarragon
1 chopped white of leek

½ pt (300 mls) soured cream
1 tsp flour
2 tsp capers, drained and chopped
1 tbs finely chopped watercress leaves
salt and black pepper

PLACE the fish in a buttered baking dish. Add the wine/cider and dot with half the butter. Season, then sprinkle on the tarragon. Cover with foil and bake near the top of the oven for 20 minutes. Melt the rest of the butter in a saucepan and sweat the chopped leeks in it for a couple of minutes. Sprinkle in the flour and, stirring continuously, cook over a low heat for a further two to three minutes. When the fish is cooked lift up the corner of the foil and pour out the fish liquid into a jug. Add this, a little at a time, to the saucepan mixture, stirring all the time. Bring to the boil and cook for a minute. Turn down the heat to low and stir in the cream, capers and chopped watercress. Mix well and pour over the fish steaks. Re-heat for a few minutes until ready to serve.

Braised shoulder of lamb

3 lb (1.4kg) shoulder of lamb, boned and rolled	8 ozs (225g) carrots, sliced
2 ozs (50g) butter	4 ozs (100g) diced turnip
8 ozs (225g) onions, peeled and chopped	2 large sticks of celery stalks, chopped
1 clove garlic, peeled and crushed	½ pt (300 mls) red wine
4 ozs (100g) lean bacon, chopped	¼ pt (150 mls) water
	1 level tsp crushed rosemary
	1 level tsp salt

HEAT butter in a large saucepan and add onions, garlic, bacon, carrots, turnip and celery. Cover pan and fry gently for 10 minutes, shaking pan frequently. Pour in the wine and water. Add the rosemary and salt. Bring to boil and place the lamb on top. Cover the saucepan and simmer very gently for about two and a half hours hours, until meat is tender. Transfer lamb to warm serving dish and surround with vegetables from saucepan. Strain liquid and pour into a clean saucepan, boil briskly until reduced by half and then pour over the meat.

Sole Veronique

4 fillets sole, skinned	2 tbs flour
1 small onion, sliced	1 pt (600 mls) milk
2 bay leaves	1 cup dry white wine
8 peppercorns	bunch of green grapes, peeled
4 tsps lemon juice	and de-pipped
2 ozs (50g) butter	salt and black pepper

ROLL up the sole fillets and secure with coctail sticks. Stand them upright in a greased ovenproof dish with the sliced onions, bay leaves, peppercorns and lemon juice. Add the wine and enough water to half cover the fish. Cover and cook in a moderate oven (180°C, gas 4) for 25 to 30 minutes, until tender. With a straining spoon carefully transfer fish to a clean, serving dish, cover with kitchen foil and keep hot. Strain half a pint of the fish liquor into a clean pan and reduce to half its original quantity by boiling fast. Melt butter in a small saucepan, stir in the flour and cook for a minute. Remove from heat and slowly add the milk and fish liquor. Return to heat, bring to the boil, stirring continuously, and simmer until smooth and thick. Pour over fish and surround with grapes.

Puddings

Royal Sussex Delight

3 eggs, separated
2 tbs castor sugar
3 drops vanilla essence
2 small tsp gelatine

2 tbs boiling water
6 tsp apricot jam
¼ pt (150 mls) double cream, whipped

BEAT the egg yolks and sugar together until the mixture is almost white, then add the vanilla essence. Beat egg whites into stiff peaks. Dissolve the gelatine in the boiling water and when cool fold it quickly into the eggs yolks and sugar mix. Fold in egg whites and pile the mixture into individual glasses or bowls. Allow to set. Carefully spoon a little apricot jam into each glass and serve with whipped cream.

Apple meringue
with Calvados

8 ozs (225g) short crust pastry
1 oz (25g) butter
2 lbs (1 kg) eating apples, peeled and sliced
3 tbs Calvados

2 eggs, separated
2 tbs castor sugar
1 tbs cornflour
¼ pt (150 mls) milk
2 ozs (50g) sifted icing sugar

ROLL out the pastry and use it to line an eight inch fluted flan dish. Prick well all over and line the pastry with kitchen foil to stop it rising during cooking. Place on a baking tray and bake in hot oven (220°C, gas 7) for 15 minutes. Remove foil and bake for a further 15 minutes until crisp and golden. Melt the butter in a frying pan and saute the apples until soft. Warm a tablespoonful of Calvados then set light to it and pour it, flaming, over the apples. Stir together the egg yolks, castor sugar and cornflour in a small saucepan. Add a little of the milk and beat until smooth. Gradually add the remaining milk and stir over a low heat until it is smooth and thick. Stir in another tablespoon of the Calvados. Spread this creamy mixture evenly over the pastry case and arrange the apples over the cream, keeping the surface level. Whisk the egg whites until stiff, stir in the icing sugar and continue to whisk until the whites stand in peaks. Spread this over the apples and fluff up with a fork. Bake in a moderate oven (170°C, gas 4) for eight minutes until meringue is golden brown. Sprinkle with remaining Calvados and serve hot.

Lemon posset

3 egg whites
1½ pts (900 mls) double cream
4 heaped tbs castor sugar

juice of 2 lemons
grated rind of 1 lemon
sherry glass white wine

WHIP egg whites until really stiff. In a separate bowl whip the cream and castor sugar together until thick. Add lemon juice and grated rind and whip again until thoroughly mixed, then stir in the wine. Finally fold in the stiff whites of eggs. Cover and put in the fridge until ready to serve.

Pineapple rice pudding
(hot or cold)

4 ozs (100g) pudding rice
1 lb (450g) can crushed pineapple, undrained
3 ozs(75g) sultanas

4 eggs, lightly beaten
½ pt (300 mls) milk
ground cinnamon or nutmeg
slices of fruit for decoration

ADD rice to a large pan of boiling water and boil, uncovered, until just tender. Drain well and combine with sultanas and undrained pineapple in a medium pudding bowl. Stir in the combined eggs and milk. Pour into a large, greased ovenproof dish and put this into a baking dish with enough hot water in it to come halfway up the sides of the ovenproof dish. Bake in a moderate oven (170°C, gas 4) for 30 minutes. Remove and sprinkle lightly with cinnamon or nutmeg, bake for a further 15 minutes, or until pudding feels firm to touch. Decorate with slices of fruit of your own choice and serve hot, or chill in fridge and serve cold.

• •

JELLY TIP: When using powdered gelatine always sprinkle it on top of the liquid, then put the container in hot water over heat until the gelatine dissolves. A pint (600 mls) of liquid or fruit juice needs 1 oz (25g) of gelatine to make it set. Half an ounce will set one pint (600 mls) of mayonnaise or a really thick sauce.

MAY....

MAY 1 was Garland Day in old Sussex. Children, hoping to earn a penny or two, would try to sell bunches of wild flowers round the houses, morris dancers were extremely active and chimney sweeps would have primroses or cowslips in their caps. Some of these old customs have survived, or been revived to benefit the organisers' favourite charities. Participants in such outdoor activities, while not actually requiring meals on the march, will want something to eat when it is over. Today one cannot send the family off with some hard boiled eggs, cheese sandwiches, an apple each and a slice of cake – certainly not if they are going to Glyndebourne. The original opera house there opened its doors for the first time on May 28 1934 and picnics par excellence have been consumed on its lawns ever since. The set picnic menus I have included are suitable for al fresco festivities anywhere.

MENUS OF THE MONTH

First courses	Main dishes	Puddings	Set picnic
Pear and blue cheese salad Consomme eggs Crab Newburg	Chicken Maryland Fillets of plaice with soft roes Pork chops with apples	Banana and apricot tarts Rhubarb crumble Orange and strawberry Chantilly	Egg mousse Salmon with horseradish ice Asparagus vinaigrette Pru's cheesecake

First courses

Pear and blue cheese salad

8 ozs (225g) blue cheese, crumbled
mayonnaise, home-made or Hellmans
4 pears, peeled, cored and halved,
lettuce
few grapes, peeled and de-pipped
chopped nuts

BLEND the crumbled cheese with enough mayonnaise to make a creamy mixture. Arrange the pear halves on a bed of lettuce and cover with the cheese mayonnaise. Garnish with grapes and chopped nuts.

Consomme eggs
(for six)

2 sticks of celery

11 oz (295g) tin of consomme

6 eggs

mayonnaise, home-made or Hellmans

chives for garnish

FINELY chop the celery and mix with the liquid consomme. Dissolve a quarter of an ounce of gelatine in a tablespoonful of boiling water and, when cool, add to the consomme. Put a little of this mixture into each of six ramekins. Softly poach the eggs and when cold trim the whites and put an egg into each ramekin, spooning over it the the remaining consomme. Put in fridge to set and serve garnished with chopped chives.

Crab Newburg

1lb (450g) crabmeat, fresh or tinned

salt and black pepper

paprika

3ozs (75g) butter

5 tbs dry sherry

¼ pt (150mls) double cream

yolks of 3 eggs

8 ozs (225g) freshly boiled rice

FRY the crab meat in butter for four or five minutes. Pour in the sherry. Simmer slowly until the liquid is reduced to half. Put cream and broken egg yolks into a double saucepan and cook, stirring continuously, until sufficiently thick to coat the back of a spoon. Do not allow to boil. Adjust seasoning to taste. Arrange hot rice on serving plates and place equal amounts of crab mix in the centre. Pour cream and egg yolk sauce over each one and sprinkle with paprika lightly before serving.

Main dishes

Chicken Maryland

3-4 lb (1.4 -1.8kg) oven ready chicken

3 tbs seasoned flour

1 beaten egg

dry breadcrumbs

2 ozs (50g) butter

2 tbs oil

4 bananas

4 rashers of streaky bacon

CUT the bird into four portions, coat each one with seasoned flour, dip in beaten egg and coat with the breadcrumbs. If the egg is a small one and the chicken portions very large you might have to use a second beaten egg. Fry the chicken in a mixture of the butter and oil, turning frequently, until the bird is lightly brown and tender. Serve the chicken with fried bananas, corn fritters (see recipe on next page), bacon rolls and a green vegetable of your choice.

Corn fritters

14 ozs (400g) can of sweet corn
4 ozs (100g) plain flour
1 tsp baking flour
2 tsp salt

pinch of paprika
2 eggs
butter for frying mixed with a little
sunflour oil

DRAIN corn thoroughly and empty into a bowl with all the dry ingredients. Add the egg yolks and beat until thick. Beat egg whites until soft, not stiff, and fold into mixture. Shape into cakes and fry.

Fillets of plaice with
soft roes and mustard sauce

2 fillets of plaice per person
2 soft roes per fillet
3 ozs (75g) butter
milk to cover fillets
salt and pepper

flour
mustard sauce
mashed potatoes
parsley to garnish

REMOVE any stringy or black pieces from the roe, wash and dry them. Dust them in flour and fry in butter for a few minutes, turning to be sure they are cooked on both sides. Put the plaice fillets flat on a board, place two roes on each one and then roll up and secure with a cocktail stick. Put the fillets in an ovenproof dish, dot each one with butter and pour over enough milk to cover them all. Cover the dish with foil and put in a moderate oven (180°C. gas 4) for 15 minutes. Remove and keep warm. Before serving pipe mashed potatoes round the fish on the dish and sprinkle with parsley. Make the mustard sauce (see recipe on page 93) and serve separately.

Pork chops with apples

4 thick pork chops,
2 ozs (50g) butter
2 eating apples, peeled, cored
and cut into pieces

2 ozs (50g) sultanas
1 tsp grated lemon peel
1/4 pt (150 mls) Madeira or sherry
salt and pepper

TRIM the chops of fat and put into an ovenproof pan with the butter and cook slowly, turning once or twice, until they are cooked through and are nicely browned on both sides. Add the remaining ingredients, put a lid on the pan and place in a moderate oven (170°C, gas 4) for 40 minutes. Transfer to a serving dish and garnish with parsley. Serve wih fried potatoes and red cabbage.

Puddings

Rhubarb crumble

1½ lbs (675g) rhubarb washed
and cut into inch pieces
2 tbs water
4 ozs (100g) light brown sugar
l level tsp of powdered ginger

For the crumble:
3 ozs (75g) of butter
6 ozs (175g) of plain flour
2 ozs (50g) of granulated sugar.

BUTTER a pie dish and put in the rhubarb with the sugar, water and ginger. Bake in a fairly hot oven (200°C, gas 6) for about 15 minutes and then remove it while you make the crumble. Rub the butter into the flour with your fingers or in the blender, and add the sugar. The mixture should be like fine breadcrumbs. Put it on top of the cooked fruit and return to the oven – still at 200°C – until the top is beginning to brown. Serve with double cream.

Banana and apricot tarts

2 sheets of ready made puff pastry
l egg, lightly beaten
l tbs apricot jam
2 bananas, skinned and thinly sliced

2 tsp lemon juice
2 tbs honey
l oz (25g) butter

BRUSH one sheet of pastry with the egg. Place the second sheet on top and cut four rounds, using a three and a half inch fluted pastry cutter. Spread jam evenly over the pastry, arrange bananas on it and brush with the combined lemon juice and honey. Dot with butter, place on a lightly greased baking tray and cook in a hot oven (220°C, gas 7) for 15 minutes until golden brown. Allow tarts to cool and serve with a blob of cream on the top of each one.

Orange and strawberry Chantilly

3 large oranges, peeled
and pith removed
12 ozs (350g) strawberries,
stalks removed
2 to 3 tbs sweet white wine or brandy

½ pt (300 mls) double cream
2 tbs milk
2 ozs (50g) sifted icing sugar
l egg white

CUT the strawberries in half and put them into individual bowls or glass dishes. Finely slice the oranges and arrange on top of the strawberries and sprinkle on the wine or brandy. Chill for at least one hour. Before serving whip the cream and milk together until thick and beat the sugar and egg white to a stiff snow and stir it in. Pile this creamy topping on to the fruit in the dishes.

Set picnic

Egg mousse

5 hard boiled eggs	4 tbs mayonnaise, home-made
1 tbs boiling water	or Hellmans
1 tbs Worcestershire Sauce	1 tbs finely chopped onion
1 tbs soy sauce	10 oz (275g) can of consomme
2 tsp anchovy essence	1/4 oz (7g) gelatine
1/2 pt (300 mls) lightly whipped	salt and pepper
double cream	1 tbs finely chopped parsley

CHOP the hard boiled eggs and mix with the onion, parsley, anchovy essence, Worcester sauce, soy sauce, mayonnaise and whipped cream. Dissolve the gelatine in the boiling water. Pour the consomme into a pint bowl and when the gelatine has cooled add it to the soup and stir thoroughly. Combine the soup with egg mixture and transfer to a greased mould, or glass bowl and chill in the fridge for at least an hour. Just before taking on the picnic turn it out on to a serving dish, easing it out gently with a spatula.

Salmon steaks with horseradish ice

1 thick salmon steak per person	1 tbs horseradish cream
2 ozs (50g) butter	freshly ground black pepper
1/4 pt (150 mls) double cream	

GENTLY saute salmon steaks in the butter with a sprinkling of pepper, turning once, until cooked through. Set aside to cool. Whip the cream, fold in the horseradish and put in a freezer tray and freeze. Pack into a wide necked thermos flask and when ready to serve, spoon the horseradish ice onto each salmon steak. A good accompaniment is:

Asparagus vinaigrette.

ALLOW six to eight thick asparagus pieces per person. Boil until tender. Drain thoroughly and pack when cool. Sprinkle with the vinaigrette (see sauces on page 93) you have brought in a screw top jar.

Pru's cheesecake

1½ lbs (675g) curd cheese
3 eggs
8 ozs (225g) castor sugar
5 fl ozs double cream, whipped
2 tbs flour

2 tbs lemon juice
few drops vanilla essence
5 digestive biscuits
5 ozs (150g) melted butter

FLATTEN and crumble biscuits with a rolling pin. Mix in melted butter and press into an eight inch loose-bottomed cake tin. Beat cheese with eggs and sugar. Fold in whipped cream, flour, lemon and vanilla. Spread on to the biscuit base. Bake in a moderate oven (180°C, gas 4) for one hour. Turn off oven and leave door ajar for 20 minutes. Remove and when cold gently turn out of the cake tin on to a serving plate.

PICNIC POINTERS: Transporting food to a picnic can present quite a problem. You do not want soup slopping about, or a creamy pudding ending up on the bottom of the picnic hamper and dribbling out on to the car seats. So choosing the right containers is all important. The wisest course of action is to place all the food you have prepared in advance in suitable lightweight containers with secure lids and leave them in the fridge until the moment of setting off. Empty ice cream cartons and plastic boxes are invaluable for this purpose – and with luck the contents will stay firm until you reach your picnic destination.

DO NOT FORGET:

1) The corkscrew if you are taking wine
2) a bottle opener for crown corks
3) the mustard
4) sugar, if anyone takes it in tea or coffee
5) plenty of sheets of kitchen towel
6) enough cutlery, plates and glasses

JUNE
·····

IF June is flaming – as tradition requires it to be – the pick-your-own season for soft fruits should be well under way. Vegetables too are there for the harvesting and it is worth an aching back to come home with sun warmed broad beans and peas in their pods. June 16 is the start of the coarse fishing season. From now until March there is a chance, albeit a slim one, that an angling friend or relative will come home with a carp of a size to be cooked rather than taken to the taxidermist for glass case treatment. Refer to Izaak Walton's *The Compleat Angler*, first published in 1562, for the recipe. Incidentally, it was a Sussex man, Leonard Mascall of Plumpton, who was credited, some say wrongly, with introducing carp to this country in Tudor times.

MENUS OF THE MONTH

First courses	Main dishes	Puddings	Set picnic
Smoked mackerel and watercress pate	Festival chicken	Strawberry or raspberry slices	Melon with prawns
Prawn and avocado salad	Smoked fish and rice slice	Chocolate cream mould	Cold chicken with tuna sauce
Chilled ratatouille	Fillets of pork Veronique	Fresh apricot mousse	Italian oranges

First courses

Smoked mackerel and watercress pate

4 ozs (100g) smoked mackerel fillets, skinned and flaked
2 ozs (50g) soft cheese
2 tbs natural yoghurt

1 tsp creamed horseradish
squeeze of lemon juice
salt and black pepper
½ bunch watercress, washed and de-stalked

BLEND watercress, mackerel, soft cheese, yoghurt, horseradish and generous grindings of black pepper until smooth. Remove to a serving dish and chill. Garnish with sprigs of watercress and serve with toast.

Prawn and avocado salad

2¼ lbs (1kg) king prawns, cooked
1 Little Gem lettuce,washed and dried
2 avocados, skinned and sliced
2 tbs chopped chives
8 fl ozs mayonnaise,

2 tbs lemon juice
1 small fresh red chilli, finely chopped
1 clove garlic, crushed
few drops tabasco sauce

ADD the lemon juice, chilli, garlic and tabasco to the mayonnaise and stir well. Shell and remove the veins from prawns. Arrange lettuce leaves on serving plates and place on top the prawns and avocado slices. Cover with mayonnaise and sprinkle with chopped chives.

Chilled ratatouille

2 onions, chopped finely
2 green peppers, halved and de-seeded
2 aubergines, chopped and salted
3 courgettes, chopped and salted

3 tomatoes, peeled and coarsely chopped
1 clove garlic, finely chopped
olive oil
2 tbs chopped parsley

HEAT oil in a thick-bottomed saucepan and cook onions gently until transparent. Dry aubergines and courgettes with kitchen paper or a cloth and add to onions with the peppers and garlic. Cover with a lid and cook on a low heat for half an hour. Add the tomatoes and cook for a further 10 minutes. Season with salt and pepper and stir in parsley. When cool, place in fridge to chill thoroughly. Serve cold.

Main dishes

Festival chicken

4 lb (1.8kg) roasting chicken
1 lemon
2 ozs (50g) butter
4 tbs white wine
1 small onion, chopped
1 tbs oil
1 tbs curry powder

¼ pt (150 mls) chicken stock from cube
1 to 2 tbs mango chutney
3 tbs apricot jam
½ pt (300 mls) double cream
¼ pt (150 mls) mayonnaise
¼ pt (150 mls) soured cream
1 red pepper, grapes and cress to garnish

SQUEEZE the lemon and place it, with a nob of butter, inside the chicken. Place in roasting dish, spread with the remaining butter and pour over the lemon juice and the wine. Roast in moderately hot oven (200°C, gas 6) for 25 minutes per lb. Baste well. Remove from oven, cool and strain off the juices into a separate bowl. When the bird is cold, remove all flesh and chop into one inch chunks. Soften onion in oil, add the curry powder and cook over a low heat for three to four minutes. Stir in the chicken juices, stock, chutney and jam. Bring to the boil and simmer for 10 minutes. Liquidise and allow to cool. Whip the cream, add the mayonnaise, soured cream and cooled curry sauce. Season. Add the chopped chicken flesh to the sauce and pile on to a serving dish, lined with lettuce. Chill, and garnish just before serving with slices of red pepper, grapes and watercress.

Smoked fish and rice slice

1¼ lbs (550g) smoked fish
1½ pts (900 mls) chicken stock, from cubes
2 tsps curry powder
8 ozs (225g) long grain rice
1 egg, lightly beaten
2 extra eggs, lightly beaten

¼ pt (150 mls) milk
¼ pt (150 mls) double cream
4 ozs (100g) grated strong Cheddar cheese
4 shallots or spring onions, chopped
1 tsp dry English mustard
2 tbs chopped parsley

BRING stock to the boil in large pan and add curry powder and rice. Reduce heat, cover and simmer for about 30 minutes, or until all the liquid has been absorbed and the rice is tender. Stir in one beaten egg. Spread the rice mixture evenly over base of an approximately 10 x 6 inch greased baking dish. Cook fish in pan of simmering water for about five minutes. Drain, flake with fork, removing all bones, and spread over the rice. Pour over the combined extra eggs, milk, cream, cheese, shallots, mustard and parsley. Bake in a moderate oven for 30 minutes, or until golden brown and set firm. Serve hot with a green vegetable of your choice or allow to rest for 10 minutes then refrigerate for two or three hours, or overnight, and serve cold.

SMOKE YOUR OWN: In Sussex one of course goes to Springs at Edburton for smoked salmon and other delicacies but such fish as haddock and trout can be smoked at home. Cut the bottom out of a 10 gallon steel drum and punch some holes in the removeable lid. Stand it on a fire of fir cones, peat, hardwood sawdust or oak chips. Gut the fish, open it up and rub inside and out with salt. Stand overnight, then hang it in the open air for three hours to dry. Suspend fish by the tail, a foot above the fire, on a wire stretched across the drum. Put on the lid, maintain an even heat, and smoke it for about 8 to 10 hours.

Fillets of pork Veronique

2 pork fillets, trimmed
24 green grapes, halved,
peeled and de-pipped
2 ozs (50g) butter
¼ pt (150 mls) white wine
¼ pt (150 mls) chicken stock from a cube
1 onion, peeled and quartered

1 carrot, scraped and sliced
1 bay leaf
¼ tsp dried thyme
1 oz (25g) butter
1 oz (25g) flour
salt and black pepper

CUT the pork fillets halfway through and open out. Smear with butter. Put 12 halved grapes down the centre of one side of each fillet and fold the other side over. Roll up and tie with string. Heat some butter and brown the rolls on all sides. Transfer to a casserole, add wine, stock, seasoning, onion and carrot, bay leaf and thyme. Cover and cook in a moderate oven (180°C gas 4) for an hour. Remove pork from the casserole, place on a heated serving dish and remove string. Strain liquid into a jug and retain. In a saucepan heat the butter, quickly add the flour and stir thoroughly. Add strained liquid, continuing to stir until well blended. Take off heat and mix a little of the sauce with the beaten egg yolk and then return to to the pan. Place on a low heat and stir while it thickens. Season to taste. Pour over fillets and decorate with remaining grapes.

Puddings

Strawberry or raspberry slices

12 ozs (350g) puff pastry
1 pt (600 mls) double cream
sugar to taste
2 tbs orange liqueur

2 lbs (900g) strawberries (or raspberries) topped and tailed
icing sugar

DIVIDE the pastry dough into three. Roll each piece into a strip of about 5 x 12 inches, and then cut the three strips into four even slices, making a dozen 5 x 3 inch slices. Trim the edges evenly and place each strip on a wet baking sheet. Prick all over and bake in a hot oven (220°C, gas 7) for 10 to 15 minuntes. Leave to cool on a wire rack. Whisk the cream and flavour with sugar and liqueur. Place four pastry strips on a flat serving dish. Spread half of the cream on to these strips and cover with half the prepared fruit. Place four more strips over these and spread with the other half of the cream, followed by rest of the fruit. Cover with the remaining four pastry strips. Press down lightly and dredge with sifted icing sugar.

Chocolate cream mould

3 tbs boiling water	*½ pt (300 mls) cold custard*
1 level tbs granulated sugar	*1 tsp vanilla essence*
3 level tsps gelatine	*3 ozs (75g) plain chocolate, grated*
½ pt (300 mls) fresh double cream	*chocolate chips or curls*

PUT water, sugar, chocolate and gelatine into a saucepan over a low heat and stir until thoroughly dissolved. Allow to cool. Whip cream until fairly stiff. Make sure there is no skin on the custard, whip until completely smooth and then whisk in the cooled gelatine mixture and add the vanilla. Fold in the whipped cream and then leave to cool, stirring occasionally, until it begins to thicken and set. Refrigerate in a lightly greased one and a half pint mould until firmly set. To turn out dip the mould in hot water and invert onto a plate. Decorate with curls or chips of chocolate.

Apricot mousse

1 lb (450g) apricots, stoned and halved	*4 egg whites*
2 oz (50g) sugar	*few peeled almonds*
1 tbs lemon juice	*1 tsp gelatine*
¼ pt (150 mls) double cream	*2 tbs water*

STEW the apricots with the sugar and water until soft. If there is more than two tablespoonfuls of juice on the surface, remove it. Puree the stewed fruit and pour into a measuring jug – there should be half a pint. Pour into a mixing bowl and stir in the lemon juice and taste. If too sour, stir in more sugar. Melt the gelatine in a quarter of a pint (150 mls) of boiling water and when dissolved pour into the fruit. Whip the cream and when the fruit mixture is cool, fold it in. Beat the egg whites into stiff peaks and fold this into the mixture. Decorate to taste.

Set Picnic

Melon with prawns

1 medium-sized ripe Cantaloupe	*½ lb (225g) fresh or de-frosted prawns*
or Galia melon	*mayonnaise, home-made or Hellmans*

SLICE the top off the melon and cut a piece from the base so that it will stay upright on its dish. Remove all the seeds and pour off any excess juice. Cut or ball the flesh into small pieces. Add the prawns, carefully fold in the mayonnaise and put mixture back into the empty melon. Replace the top, and refrigerate, carefully wrapped in cling film so it does not flavour other food, until required.

Cold chicken with tuna sauce

2 tbs oil

4 chicken breasts

For the sauce:

4 tbs oil

1 egg yolk

3 ozs (75g) tin tuna in oil

2 tbs lemon juice

2½ fl ozs double cream

salt and white pepper

half a chicken stock cube

chopped parsley, capers and stoned

black olives for garnish

DISSOLVE the chicken stock cube in quarter of a pint (150 mls) of boiling water and allow to get cold. Cook the chicken fillets in the oil in a pan on top of the stove, turning once or twice to be sure they a cooked through. Allow to get cold. Blend all the ingredients for the sauce in a liquidiser until pureed to the consistency of thick cream. If it is too stiff after blending, thin down with the cold chicken stock until there is sufficient smooth thick sauce to cover the chicken in the dish. Garnish with chopped parsley, a few stoned black olives and scatter a few capers over the top.

Italian oranges

6 good eating oranges

juice of 2 oranges

2 tbs red colouring

½ lb (225g) sugar

1 tbs of brandy

1 tbs orange Curaçao

(this recipe must be made the day before serving)

SHRED the peel from the oranges finely with a potato peeler and put it in a pan and cover with the sugar, orange juice, colouring and alcohol. Simmer for 30 minutes. Tip into a bowl and leave to marinate for at least 12 hours. It should be thick and a good bright red. Cut away all the white pith from the peeled oranges and slice across into thick rounds. Cover with cling film and refrigerate overnight. When ready to serve pour the red sauce over the top at the last moment. Serve with cream.

• •

BARBECUES

BARBECUES have come to Britain from sunnier and warmer climes. Australians plan them weeks ahead, knowing their weather will be wonderful. It is a little different in Sussex. It is only necessary to think of inviting a few friends to chew a chop cooked on the charcoal of your brand new barby and low pressure systems queue up in the Channel to rain it off.

Here any successful sizzles are the spontaneous ones. A dash round the supermarket shelves in the morning will produce enough easy-to-grill burgers, drumsticks, chops and cuts of meat for father to show off his cooking skills to the family in the evening. This he can do either in the garden at home or on the beach, if

a) your barbecue is portable

b) there is a beach nearby and

c) the tide is right.

More elaborate out-of-doors cooking needs more elaborate preparation. Most of it can be done indoors – and a day or two ahead. Here are some dishes that can appear at the fireside looking as if they were cooked there, and a foil wrapped bundle to put on the glowing coals. . .

Maple spare ribs

4 lbs (1.8kg) pork spare ribs cut into 2 rib pieces	2 cloves garlic, peeled and crushed
5 fl ozs maple syrup	2 tbs tomato puree
1/4 tsp cayenne pepper	1 tbs prepared mustard
	2 tbs lemon juice

MIX all the ingredients together except the meat. Put the ribs into a roasting tin and cook in a hot oven (220°C, gas 7) for half an hour. Pour off the fat, return the ribs to the tin and pour over the maple syrup mixture. Reduce oven heat to moderate (180°C, gas 4) and cook for a further 45 minutes. Transfer to a serving plate and spoon over the ribs any sauce lying at the bottom of the roasting pan. Allow to cool enough to eat with the fingers.

Cheese and herb drumsticks

8 chicken drumsticks
½ oz (14g) butter, melted
For cheese and herb seasoning:
½ oz (14g) butter
3 shallots or spring
onions, finely chopped

1 clove garlic, crushed
1 tbs chopped fresh basil
2¼ ozs (56g) Ricotta cheese
1 tbs grated Parmesan
1 tbs dry breadcrumbs
1 egg yolk

HEAT butter in pan, add shallots and garlic and cook for a minute, stirring. Remove from heat and stir in the basil, cheeses, breadcrumbs and egg yolk. Mix well and allow to cool. Loosen the skin around the drumsticks and push approximately one tablespoonful of the cooled mixture in the space you have created. Pull the skin back over the filling and place the drumsticks on a greased baking dish. Brush them with butter and bake in moderate oven (180°C, gas 4) for about 45 minutes, or until chicken is tender and well browned. Serve round the fire or allow them to cool and keep in the fridge to heat up later on the barbecue.

Trout bundles

Allow half a trout per person
4 ozs (100g) butter
lemon juice

chopped parsley
black pepper

TOP and tail the fish and remove their backbones. Divide the butter into one ounce portions and with each pat grease a sheet of foil and spread the rest of the butter over the inside of the fish. Season with pepper and lemon juice, sprinkle with parsley and close up the fish and parcel it in the buttered foil. Cook for 10 minutes in the hot ashes, or on the side of the coals. Pass round the parcels so guests can eat with their fingers.

Barbecue sauce

5 tbs olive oil
1 medium onion, peeled and chopped
1 heaped tbs sugar
1½ tbs Worcester sauce
5 tbs tomato ketchup

6 tbs water
1 tbs prepared mustard
½ tsp salt,
juice of 1 lemon
pepper

COOK the onion in the oil until it is soft and transparent. Add the remaining ingredients and simmer for 15 minutes. This makes half a pint of sauce for basting and to serve with barbecued chicken, steaks, burgers and lamb chops.

JULY
·······

FOR hundreds of years a horned sheep has been roasted whole in the West Sussex village of Ebernoe on, or near, July 25, which is St James's Day. The horns go to the highest scorer in the cricket match played on the common and the rest of the animal is eaten at so much a slice – the proceeds going to charity. With any roast there is always some meat left over. Why not use it to make a herby meat loaf, which is equally good, hot or cold?

MENUS FOR THE MONTH			
First courses	**Main dishes**	**Puddings**	**Set picnic**
Chilled gazpacho	Herby meat loaf	Fruity fool	Crab mayonnaise
Avocado and cheese dip	Baked whiting with prawns	Coffee fudge cream pie	Duck and ham loaf
Parma ham pate	Galantine of guinea fowl	Maxine's lemon curd pudding	Mushroom salad Raspberry cream and orange

First courses

Chilled gazpacho

4 slices of stale brown bread
sufficient oil to soak breadcrumbs
3 cloves garlic, crushed
salt and 12 grindings black pepper
4 tbs red wine vinegar
14 ozs (400g) tin of peeled
whole tomatoes

1 oz (25g) castor sugar)
8 oz (225g) tin pimentos
454 ml jar Libby's tomato juice
1/4 red pepper, chopped finely
handful of parsley, chopped
1/4 cucumber, peeled and chopped
croutons

AFTER removing crusts, make breadcrumbs by hand or in food processor and put them into a large bowl and cover with oil. Mix until well blended. Add crushed garlic, stir in wine vinegar. Blend tomatoes, pimentoes and tomato juice together until pureed, pour onto crumbs and stir well. Add sugar and seasoning. Cover with cling film and refrigerate, preferably overnight. Serve, accompanied by dishes of chopped cucumber and croutons.

Avocado and cheese dip

1 avocado
11 ozs (300g) soured cream

2 ozs (50g) strong Cheddar,grated
1/4 tsp chilli powder

BLEND all the ingredients together until smooth. Transfer to a serving bowl and refrigerate until required. The dip can be used with celery, crisps or gulls' eggs.

Parma ham pate

8 ozs (225g) Parma ham
1/4 pt (150 mls) double cream
1/4 pt (150 mls) single cream
freshly ground white pepper
squeeze lemon juice

3 tbs dry white wine
1 sachet gelatine
2 egg whites
extra ham and watercress
sprigs for decoration

CHOP the ham very finely in a food processor, add the creams and blend again until it becomes a rough paste. Transfer to mixing bowl and season generously with white pepper and stir in lemon juice. Heat white wine, add gelatine and stir until dissolved. Allow to cool slightly and then stir into ham mixture. Whisk egg whites until stiff peaks form. Using a metal spoon carefully fold whites into ham. Spoon the pate mixture into a lightly oiled ring mould and smooth the top. Leave in the fridge for a couple of hours. When set turn out on to a serving dish and decorate the centre with watercress sprigs and chopped Parma ham.

Main dishes

Herby meat loaf

1lb (450g) lean minced lamb
3 ozs (75g) dried breadcrumbs
1 egg, beaten
1 small onion, peeled and sliced
4 tsps Worcestershire sauce

2 tbs tomato puree
2 tsp dry English mustard
2 tbs chopped fresh mixed herbs,
or 1 tsp dried
salt and freshly ground black pepper

PRE-HEAT oven to 190°C, gas 5. Lightly grease a pint loaf tin and put in 1 tbs of the breadcrumbs. Shake around to coat tin thoroughly. Mix the lamb, egg, onion, Worcestershire Sauce, tomato puree, mustard, mixed herbs and seasoning to taste, and spoon into the tin. Smooth top. Bake in the oven for 25 to 30 minutes, until cooked. To test pierce with a meat skewer. If it comes out clean the loaf is cooked. Remove from oven and rest for about five minutes before turning out. Serve hot or cold with home-made tomato sauce (see recipe page 92)

Baked whiting stuffed
with prawns

1 fish per person, cleaned and boned
juice of a lemon
salt and black pepper
6 tbs parsley, chopped

10 ozs (275g) button mushrooms, sliced
10 ozs (275g) prawns, shelled
4 ozs (100g) butter

RUB the inside of each fish with salt and pepper and sprinkle the outside with lemon juice. Melt an ounce of the butter in a frying pan, add the mushrooms and fry for two to three minutes. Stir in the prawns and parsley and continue to cook for another two to three minutes. Stuff the cavities of the fish with the mushroom mixture and put them, side by side, in an ovenproof dish. Dot with the remaining butter and bake in a moderate oven (170°C, gas 4) for about 25 minutes or until the fish is cooked.

Galantine of
guinea fowl

1 guinea fowl
2 tbs oil
2 cloves garlic, crushed
2 small courgettes, topped, tailed and diced
1 onion, peeled and finely diced
4 ozs button mushrooms,
washed, dried and finely chopped

6 slices white crustless bread,
made into crumbs
juice of half a lime
2 tbs finely chopped parsley
small jar cranberry sauce
salt and fresh ground black pepper

HEAT oil in a frying pan and fry onion and garlic until soft and transparent. Remove from pan and put on one side. Fry diced courgettes and mushrooms for a few minutes. Mix these ingredients together in a bowl and add the lime juice and parsley. Season with salt and pepper. Allow to cool. Fill the breast cavity of the bird with this stuffing. Tie the legs to the body with string so it is tidy. Brush with oil and put in a baking dish. Roast on the middle shelf of the oven, at moderate heat (180°C, gas 4) for one hour, or until brown and with no blood appearing when pierced with a sharp knife. Remove and chill. Serve in slices with cranberry sauce and with the mushroom, mint and horseradish salad in the set picnic menu on page 51.

Puddings

Fruity fool

1 lb (450g) fresh fruits in season
½ pt (300mls) milk
2 tbs castor sugar
2 tbs custard powder

¼ pt (150 mls) double cream
2 ozs ratafia biscuits
8 extra ratafias for decoration

STEW fresh fruit with the sugar and allow to cool. When cold put into a liquidiser and puree. Make half a pint of custard and when it is cold combine with the pureed fruit and mix well. Whip the cream and add to the fruit and custard. Chill thoroughly. Roughly crumble the ratafias and just before serving add them to the mixture. Use one or two whole ratafia biscuits to decorate each portion.

Coffee fudge cream pie

Short crust pastry
2 level tbs apricot jam
3 ozs (75g) butter
3 ozs castor sugar
1 egg, beaten

1½ ozs (40g) walnuts, shelled
and finely chopped
8 ozs (225g) self-raising flour, sifted
2 dsps liquid coffee essence
1 dsp cold milk

ROLL out pastry and use it to line an eight inch flan dish. Spread the pastry base with the jam. In a mixing bowl, cream butter and sugar together until light and fluffy and beat in egg and walnuts. Fold in flour, coffee essence and milk. Transfer to pastry case and smooth the top with a knife. Put on a baking tray and place in the centre of a hot oven (220°C, gas 7) and bake for 15 minutes. Reduce temperature to moderate (160°C, gas 3) and bake for a further 25 to 30 minutes. Remove from oven, cover with soured cream and then return to oven for a further two minutes. Best served cold.

Maxine's lemon curd pudding

4 tbs Losely set yoghurt
4 tbs lemon curd
4 scoops vanilla ice cream

4 tbs double cream, whipped
4 quarters freshly cut lemon

TAKE four glass dessert bowls or four tall glasses and put a tablespoonful of each ingredient in each one. Garnish with quarters of lemon cut and fixed on the side of each bowl or glass.

Set picnic

Crab and cucumber mayonnaise

1 large crab	salt and pepper
1 large cucumber	pinch of paprika
7 fl ozs single cream	pinch of cayenne
squeeze of lemon juice	

PEEL cucumber and cut into half inch cubes. Put them into a small pan of boiling, salted water and cook fast for five minutes. Drain and cool. Remove crab meat from shell and mix with the cooled cucumber. Gently mix the lemon juice, salt, pepper, paprika and cayenne with the cream and in turn mix this in with the crab and cucumber. Transfer to a suitable picnic container and chill until required.

Duck and ham loaf

6 ozs (175g) cooked minced duck meat	1 small onion, peeled and minced
6 ozs (175g) lean minced ham	1/2 level tsp dried sage
4 ozs (100g) fresh white breadcrumbs	2 level tbs finely chopped parsley
1/2 level tsp orange peel, finely grated	2 large eggs, beaten
3 ozs (75g) mushrooms and stalks,	1/4 pt (150 mls) milk
washed, dried and finely chopped	salt and black pepper

COMBINE the duck, ham, breadcrumbs, orange peel, onion, mushrooms, sage and parsley. Add the beaten eggs and milk, season to taste and mix well. Transfer to a well-buttered two pound loaf tin and smooth the top with a knife. Bake in the centre of a moderate oven, (180°C, gas 4) for one hour until firm. To test, pierce with a meat skewer and if it comes out clean the loaf is ready. Leave to rest for 10 minutes then turn out on to a suitable container and cool.

Mushroom salad
with minty horseradish sauce

12 ozs button mushrooms	1 tbs finely chopped mint
2 tbs creamed horseradish	salt and pepper
3-4 tbs natural yoghurt	

Wash and carefully wipe dry the mushrooms then cut them into quarters. Mix together the horseradish, yoghurt and mint and season to taste. Mix into the mushrooms and garnish with mint before serving.

Raspberry cream
and orange

1¹/₂ lbs (675g) raspberries
2 large oranges, peeled
and pith removed
2 tbs castor sugar
¹/₂ pt (300 mls) double cream

¹/₄ pt (150 mls) natural yoghurt
2 tbs icing sugar
1 sliver of orange peel,
finely shredded, for garnish

RESERVE 10 raspberries and the shredded sliver of orange peel. Slice one of the oranges and combine with a pound of the raspberries and cover with castor sugar. Place in a suitable picnic container. Extract the juice from the remaining raspberries by crushing the fruit through a sieve. Discard seeds. Squeeze the juice from the second orange. Whip together the raspberry juice, orange juice, cream, yoghurt and icing sugar until thick and stiff. Pile on top of the raspberries and orange slices. Refrigerate for two hours. Just before packing up decorate with reserved raspberries and shredded orange peel.

• •

PICNIC PACKING: The availability of ice packs in cold bags and boxes; wine coolers that are easily portable; cardboard or plastic plates, cups and glasses has transformed picnic outings. Every device for keeping food and drink cool and safe is now to hand.

To prevent cutlery rattling around wrap it in the napkins and put an elastic band round each bundle. Take a couple of lidded empty ice cream cartons on the picnic. They are invaluable for bringing home the leftovers and the dirty knives, forks and spoons. It is also a good idea to take an empty plastic bag for the rubbish.

AUGUST
••••••••

THE court of Queen Elizabeth I was at Cowdray for a week in August 1591. The extent and splendour of the hospitality dispensed by Lord Montague was lavish in the extreme. Thirty oxen and 140 geese were consumed – and that was just at breakfast. Fortunately for present day Sussex hosts, guests do not now come quite so accompanied.

August 12 is the start of the grouse shooting season but that is on the moors of the north. Here in the south we have duck, fine fish and the soft fruits of late summer.

MENUS FOR THE MONTH

First courses	Main dishes	Puddings	Set picnic
Fishysoisse	Duck with black	Summer	Prunella's
Chicken liver	cherry sauce	pudding	terrine
pate	Lemon sole	Chocolate	Smoked salmon
Salmon and	with bananas	Cusinier	mousse
watercress	Lamb potato	Custard tart	Iced peaches
roulade	pastry pie		

First courses

Fishysoisse

2 ozs (50g) butter
8 leeks, peeled and cut into 2 inch pieces
8 ozs (225g) potatoes, peeled and sliced
15 ozs (425g) can of pink salmon,
boned, skinned and the juice reserved

1 medium onion, peeled and finely chopped
1½ pts (900 mls) chicken stock
salt and black pepper
½ pt (300 mls) milk
pinch of nutmeg

MELT the butter in a pan and sweat the leeks and potatoes in it for about 15 minutes over a low heat. Add a pint of the stock, salt and pepper and simmer, with the lid half on the pan, until the vegetables are soft. Add the salmon and the reserved juice. Stir, and transfer to a liquidiser and blend until smooth. Add the remaining stock and milk, return to the pan and heat up, if serving hot, or refrigerate if serving cold. In either case add a spoonful of cream to each serving and garnish with chopped parsley.

Chicken liver pate
with redcurrants

3 ozs (75g) butter
1 large onion, chopped finely
8 ozs (225g) chicken livers,
cleaned and chopped
8 juniper berries, crushed

1 clove garlic, crushed
2 ozs (50g) redcurrants, topped and tailed
salt
10 grindings of black pepper
melted butter to seal

MELT half the butter and cook the onions and garlic until soft. Add the livers and redcurrants and cook for five minutes, constantly stirring. Remove from heat and allow to cool. Put the mixture into the liquidizer and blend until smooth. Turn into a bowl and add the remaining butter, crushed juniper berries and seasoning. Stir thoroughly. Transfer to a bowl, smooth the surface and pour over the melted butter. Refrigerate until required.

Salmon and watercress
roulade

2 bunches watercress
7 ozs (200g) can salmon, drained
and skin and bone removed
4 ozs (100g) full fat curd cheese
3 eggs, separated
4 tbs thick mayonnaise

3 tbs plain flour
grated rind of half a lemon
1/4 pt (150 mls) single cream
salt and ground black pepper
1 lemon, quartered, for garnish

WASH watercress and discard the stalks. Reserve a few sprigs for garnish. Put the remaining leaves into the liquidiser with the salmon, flour, lemon rind, cheese, cream, egg yolks, salt and pepper. Blend until smooth, but NOT sloppy, then pour into a bowl. Whisk the egg whites until formed into soft peaks. Fold into the salmon mixture. Spread the mixture evenly into a shallow baking tin, lined with greased greaseproof paper. Bake in a pre-heated moderate oven (180°C, gas mark 4) for approximately half an hour, until the mixture is spongy to the touch but fairly firm. Turn it out immediately on to a damp, clean cloth and remove the lining paper. Spread the sponge with mayonnaise and roll it up in the cloth, as for a Swiss roll. Chill before serving, garnished with sprigs of watercress.

••••••••••••••••••••

Main dishes

Duck with black cherry sauce

lb (2.2kg) duckling
14 ozs tin (400g) of black
cherries, stoned
1 tbs lemon juice

2 tbs Madeira or sherry
4 tbs arrowroot
pinch of salt
8 grindings of black pepper

RUB salt and pepper over the bird and prick the breast all over with a fork. Put on a wire rack in a meat pan so that it does not sit in its own juices and cook in a hot oven (220°C, gas 7) for 15 minutes, or until the skin begins to brown. Then reduce the heat to moderate (180°C, gas 4) and turn the bird breast downwards and cook for about an hour or until no blood runs out when pierced with a fork. Keep hot until you have made the sauce, which should be handed separately.

Strain the juice from the cherries into a bowl and add the lemon juice, Madeira or sherry and the arrowroot. Put a pan over a slow heat and slowly pour in the contents of the bowl and stir until it has thickened, then add the cherries and keep hot until ready to serve. Red cabbage and roast potatoes go nicely with this dish.

Lemon sole or plaice with bananas

4 large fillets of plaice or lemon sole
2 ozs (50g) melted butter
2 bananas, sliced

3 ozs (75g) butter
2 ozs blanched almonds
juice of a lemon

BRUSH the fillets with melted butter and place in a buttered ovenproof dish. Cover and bake in a moderate oven (180°C, gas 4) for 15 minutes, or until opaque. Remove and place on heated serving dish. Gently fry banana slices in two ounces of the butter for two to three minutes. Arrange across fillet. Brown the remaining butter and stir in almonds and lemon juice. Pour over the fish and serve.

FISH TIPS: Do not overcook fish or it will be tough and dry. It is cooked when the flesh becomes opaque, flakes readily and can be easily pierced with a fork. Do not thaw frozen fish before cooking, except when this is necessary for ease of handling.

Lamb and potato pastry pie

4 ozs (100g) self raising flour
2 ozs (50g) dripping
1 lb (450g) cooked cold lamb
8 ozs (225g) mashed potatoes
salt and pepper

½ pt (300 mls) chicken stock
2 small onions, finely chopped
2 ozs (50g) mushrooms,
cleaned and chopped
1 egg yolk mixed with a little milk

PUT flour into a basin and rub in the dripping and then add the potato and a little water. Make this paste into a ball with floured hands and roll out a quarter of an inch thick to cover a well greased pie plate or tin. Saute the onion and mushrooms until soft and add pepper and salt to taste. Chop up the lamb, combine with the stock and onion and mushroom mixture and put on the pastry base. Cover with remaining pastry and seal the edge all the way round, mark out and paint with egg and milk. Bake in a moderate oven (180°C, gas 4) for half an hour or until the pastry looks thoroughly cooked through.

Puddings

Chocolate Cusinier

4 ozs (100g) plain dark chocolate
2 tbs water
¾ pt (450 mls) double cream
1 tbs castor sugar

2 egg yolks
rind of an orange, grated
½ to 1 tbs Cointreau

BREAK the chocolate into pieces and melt it with the water in a double boiler or heavy saucepan. Bring the cream to just below boiling point, add the melted chocolate and stir the two together well. Beat the sugar and egg yolks thoroughly and add slowly to the chocolate mixture. Add the finely grated orange rind and the Cointreau. Stir continuously over a very low heat until the mixture thickens. Put it in individual glasses, or custard cups, and chill. Garnish with a blob of cream.

Summer pudding

6-8 slices stale white bread,
crusts removed
8 ozs (225g) raspberries
8 ozs (225g) blackcurrants

8 ozs (225g) redcurrants
6 ozs (175g) castor sugar
enough water to cover the fruit

LINE a one and a half pint pudding basin with the bread, making sure there are no gaps. Simmer the fruit with the sugar and water and when cooked, allow to cool. Put the fruit into the lined basin and cover the top completely with rest of the bread. Put a saucer on top which just fits inside the rim. Weight it down, stand on a plate in case the liquid over-flows, and refrigerate overnight. Serve with a bowl of cream.

Custard tart

Short crust pastry	*yolk of 1 egg*
1 level tbs fresh white bread crumbs	*1 oz (25g) castor sugar*
½ pt luke warm milk	*grated nutmeg*
2 whole eggs	

ROLL out the pastry and use to line an eight inch buttered pie plate or tin. Sprinkle the base of the pastry with breadcrumbs. Beat the milk with the two eggs, one egg yolk and sugar. Whisk vigorously and pour the mixture into the pastry-lined pie plate or tin. Sprinkle top with nut-meg, put on a baking tray, place in centre of fairly hot oven (200° gas 6) and bake for 15 minutes. Then reduce temperature to moderate (170°C, gas 4) and bake for a further 30 to 45 minutes until the custard is set.

Set picnic

Prunella's terrine

1½ lbs (675g) fresh belly of pork	*1½ lbs (675g) lamb's liver*
1 large onion	*1 egg, beaten*
bouquet garni	*2 tbs white wine*
salt and pepper	*4 large cloves garlic, crushed*
1 lb (450g) pork sausage meat	*4 bay leaves*

CUT the rind off the pork and keep on one side with the bay leaves. Put the rindless pork, onion, sausage meat and lambs liver into a processor and blend thoroughly. Add the beaten egg, salt, pepper, crushed garlic and white wine to moisten and blend again until thoroughly mixed. Grease a terrine or loaf tin and put in all the ingredients. Cover with streaky bacon and then lay the bay leaves across the top with the pork rinds. Cover with foil and then place the terrine in a meat dish with enough water in the bottom to come half way up the terrine. Bake in a medium oven for one and a half hours. To test for readiness pierce with a meat skewer; if it comes out clean the terrine is ready. If not, cook a little longer. Allow to cool before placing in the fridge.

Smoked salmon mousse

12 ozs (350g) smoked salmon
1 pt (600 mls) mayonnaise
½ oz (14g) powdered gelatine
lemon juice
2ozs (50g) double cream
½ oz (14g) flour

½ oz (14g) butter
6 fl oz milk
1 small cucumber
1 jar red lump fish roe
1 bunch watercress
salt and pepper

LIGHTLY oil ramekin dishes or small individual moulds. Mix lemon juice with enough boiling water to make three tablespoonfuls of liquid and dissolve the gelatine in it. Prepare sauce by melting butter and, when hot, add flour. Stir together well and blend in the milk gradually. Put back on to the heat and bring to the boil to thicken. Allow to cool slightly. Chop the smoked salmon roughly and put into a food processor with half the mayonnaise. Add seasonings and prepared sauce. Process until smooth and, with the machine still running, pour in the melted gelatine. Add the cream and place in fridge. When nearly set, whisk egg white until stiff, but not dry, and fold into the mixture. Put into individual moulds and chill until firm. Meanwhile prepare green mayonnaise. Wash watercress leaves, remove stalks, chop roughly and put into food processor. Add the other half of the mayonnaise, seasonings and lemon juice to taste and blend until a good green colour. Turn mousse out onto individual plates, pour green mayonnaise over each portion and put a slice of cucumber and a little red lump fish roe on top.

Iced peaches

8 ozs (225g) crushed macaroons
5 fl ozs double cream, stiffly whipped
large tin of peach halves
2 fl ozs Kirsch

2 tsp soft brown sugar
1 tsp arrowroot dissolved
in 1 tbs warm water
½ tsp cinnamon

IN a small mixing bowl combine the crushed macaroons and 4 fl ozs of the cream. Press the mixture into the bottom of a deep, suitable picnic container. Drain the peaches and reserve the liquid. Arrange the peach halves on top of the macaroon mixture and set aside. In a small saucepan, mix together the Kirsch, sugar, cinnamon, arrowroot and four fluid ounces of peach juice. Set the pan over a moderate heat and cook, stirring constantly for about eight minutes, or until the sauce is thick and smooth. Remove the pan from the heat and pour the sauce evenly over the peach halves in the container. Fill a forcing bag, fitted with a small star-shaped nozzle, with the remaining cream and pipe it decoratively around the peaches. Chill in the fridge for an hour before packing.

SEPTEMBER
·············

MUSHROOMS in the early morning, blackberries warmed by the afternoon sun – all are here for the harvesting this month if you know where to go. At one time it was possible to find truffles beneath the beech trees on the lower slopes of the Downs and a happy hunting ground for these delectable fungi was the woods at Patching, near Worthing. In the farm shops and outside cottages in the country look out for locally grown marrows, corn on the cob, the last of the runner beans and ripe apples and pears from the orchards.

MENUS FOR THE MONTH		
First courses	**Main dishes**	**Puddings**
Artichoke hearts with cream	Blanquette of chicken	Honeycomb mould
Tuna pate	Fillet of pork with apples and cream	Elizabeth's apple snow
Cucumber and cheese mousse	Sussex beef stew	Chocolate mousse
Prawn cocktail	Chicken and mushroom kedgeree	Blackberry and apple pudding

First courses

Artichoke hearts with cream

2 ozs (50g) butter	8 fl ozs double cream
12 artichoke hearts, tinned	1 tbs lemon juice
1 tsp salt	½ tsp grated nutmeg
½ tsp white pepper	

IN a medium-sized saucepan heat the butter, add the artichokes and stir well. Add some salt and pepper and reduce heat to very low. In another small pan bring the cream to just below boiling point and add remaining salt and pepper and lemon juice. Simmer for three minutes, stirring constantly. Remove artichokes from heat and put into serving dish or individual ramekins. Pour over cream sauce and sprinkle with nutmeg.

Tuna pate

7 oz (200g) tin of tuna
4 level tbs mayonnaise
6 drops tabasco
1 level tsp capers, chopped

1 tsp lemon juice
2 ozs (50g) melted butter
black pepper
1 bay leaf, for garnish

DRAIN tuna and break up with a fork into a bowl. Add mayonnaise, tabasco, capers, lemon juice, black pepper and half the melted butter and beat with a fork until smooth. Spoon the mixture into a shallow serving dish and smooth top with a knife. Decorate with a bay leaf and then pour over the remaining butter. Refrigerate until needed.

Cucumber and cheese mousse

½ green pepper, finely chopped
½ large cucumber, skinned and chopped
8 ozs (225g) Philadelphia cream cheese
1 tsp juice of a grated onion
salt and white pepper
½ pt (300 mls) chicken stock

½ oz (14g) gelatine
2 tbs white wine vinegar
1 tbs castor sugar
pinch of ground mace or coriander
¼ pt (150 mls) double cream, whipped
watercress for garnish

OIL a ring mould. Work the cheese with the onion juice and seasoning. Dissolve gelatine in three tablespoonfuls of chicken stock and add to the cheese mixture. Stir in the rest of the stock. Drain the chopped cucumber and pepper and mix with the vinegar, sugar and spice. When the cheese mixture is cold fold in the cucumber and pepper and then the whipped cream. Pour into the ring mould and refrigerate for at least four hours. Turn out onto a serving dish and arrange the watercress in the centre.

Percy's prawn cocktail

8 ozs (225g) shelled prawns
4 king prawns for garnish
5-6 lettuce leaves
4 lemons wedges
2 tbs whipped double cream

chopped parsley
4 heaped tbs mayonnaise
1 level tbs tomato puree
1 tsp Worcestershire Sauce
2 tsp lemon juice

ADD the tomato puree, Worcester Sauce and lemon juice to the mayonnaise, mix well and fold in the whipped cream. Add the prawns to the sauce and mix well. Shred the lettuce finely and divide equally on to four plates, bowls or goblets. Place equal amounts of the prawn mixture on to the lettuce and sprinkle with chopped parsley. Garnish with a king prawn and a wedge of lemon. Serve with brown bread and butter.

Main dishes

Blanquette of chicken

3-4 lb (1.4kg-1.8kg) roasting chicken	4 cloves
½ pt (300 mls) stock or water	¼ level tsp mixed herbs
½ pt (300 mls) milk	½ level tsp salt
4 ozs (100g) streaky bacon, chopped	1 oz (25g) butter
2 egg yolks	1 oz (25g) flour
2 tsp lemon juice	To garnish: 4 rashers streaky bacon,
¼ level tsp grated nutmeg	halved, rolled and grilled
2 ozs (50g) mushrooms and stalks	4 lemon wedges
1 large onion	1 level tbs finely chopped parsley

CUT chicken into eight pieces and put into a large saucepan with the stock (or water) and milk. Add the chopped bacon. Press cloves into the onion and add to pan with nutmeg, mushrooms and stalks, herbs and salt and bring to the boil. Remove any scum and lower the heat. Cover pan and simmer gently for about one and a half hours, until chicken is tender. Strain the liquid and reserve. Transfer chicken to warm serving dish and keep hot. Melt butter in a clean saucepan, add flour and cook for two minutes without browning. Gradually blend in the chicken liquor and cook, stirring, until the sauce comes to the boil and thickens. Simmer for two minutes, remove from heat and cool slightly. Stir in egg yolks and lemon juice and pour over the chicken.

Fillet of pork with apples and cream

4 Granny Smith apples, peeled,	4 ozs (100g) butter
cored and diced	2 shallots or spring onions, sliced
8 ozs (225g) pork fillets	4 tbs Calvados
salt and fresh ground black pepper	6 tbs double cream

STEW the apple cubes gently in a little water in a covered saucepan. Remove any fat from the pork, then season and slice into eight pieces. Heat butter in a frying pan and just as it begins to turn brown, put in the pork slices and fry for three to four minutes on each side, until tender. Reduce the heat and fry for three more minutes on each side. Place in a hot serving dish and keep warm. Fry the sliced onions/shallots in the pan. Warm the Calvados, pour into the pan and set alight. Mash the cooked apples and add to the pan with the cream, stirring constantly to make a smooth sauce. Season to taste with salt and pepper. Pour the sauce over the meat and serve immediately.

Sussex beef stew

1 lb (450g) braising steak,
trimmed and cut into cubes
2 tbs oil
2 onions, peeled and diced
1 carrot, scraped and diced
1 turnip, peeled and diced

2 ozs (50g) pearl barley
1 tbs Worcestershire Sauce
¾ pt (450 mls) stock
2 bay leaves
salt and black pepper
sprigs of parsley for garnish

HEAT the oil in a frying pan and brown the meat. Reduce heat, add vegetables and cook for about three minutes. Transfer to a casserole and add the remaining ingredients. Cover and cook for one and a half hours in a moderate oven (180°C, gas 4). Adjust seasoning to taste. Remove bay leaves and serve garnished with parsley.

Chicken and mushroom kedgeree

6 ozs (175g) chicken, cooked,
boned and chopped up
6 ozs (175g) long-grain rice
4 hard-boiled eggs, shelled
and roughly chopped
3 ozs (75g) butter

4 ozs(100g) button mushrooms,
washed, dried and sliced
4 tbs double cream
freshly ground black pepper
2 tbs chopped fresh parsley

COOK the rice in boiling salted water for about 10 minutes until tender. Drain. Melt butter in large frying pan and add sliced mushrooms. Cook gently for about four minutes until soft. Add rice, chopped chicken, double cream, chopped egg and salt and pepper to taste, stir together and heat through and serve sprinkled with chopped parsley.

Puddings

Honeycomb mould

2 large eggs, separated
1 pt (600 mls) milk
3 tbs sugar

few drops vanilla essence
4 tsp powdered gelatine
2 tbs boiling water

MAKE a custard with the egg yolks, milk and sugar and flavour with vanilla, then leave to cool. Dissolve the gelatine in the boiling water and add to the custard. Cool. Whisk the egg whites very stiffly and fold them lightly into the cool custard mixture. Pour into a glass dish or mould, put into the fridge to set. When required turn out onto a serving dish and serve with a chocolate sauce, or with stewed fruit, or jam and cream

Elizabeth's apple snow

6 large apples, peeled,
cored and sliced
¼ pt (150 mls) double cream
2 ozs (50g) castor sugar

2 cloves
pinch cinnamon
1 squeeze lemon juice
2 tbs water

STEW the apples, sugar, cloves and lemon juice in the water until soft. Take them off the heat, remove the cloves, and mash the apple with a wooden spoon until nearly a puree. Transfer to a mixing bowl, put in the pinch of cinnamon and stir well. Set on one side to cool. Whip the cream until stiff and fold into the apple puree. Refrigerate for several hours, until really firm. Decorate with a twist of lemon peel.

Chocolate mousse

4 eggs, separated
8 ozs (225g) plain dark chocolate
1 tbs warm water

1 tbs brandy
cream and grated chocolate
for decoration

BREAK chocolate into small pieces and melt slowly in a heatproof bowl over a pan of gently simmering water. When melted stir in the egg yolks, one at a time, and then the warm water and brandy. Remove from heat and allow to cool. Whisk the eggs whites until very stiff and fold into the cool chocolate. Pour into small individual dishes or mousse pots. Cover with cling film and refrigerate overnight. When ready to serve pour a thin layer of cream on top of each mousse, and sprinkle with grated chocolate.

Blackberry and apple pudding

6 large slices of stale white bread
5 tbs water
4 ozs (100g) granulated sugar
1 lb (450g) fresh blackberries, washed

2 cooking apples, peeled
cored and sliced
½ pt (150 mls) double cream

REMOVE crusts from bread and use three or four slices to line, without gaps, a lightly greased two pint pudding basin. Melt the sugar slowly in the water in a pan, add the fruit and simmer gently for about 10 to 15 minutes. Pour the fruit and juice into the pudding basin and cover the top with the remaining bread slices. Put the basin on a plate, as juices may overflow, and cover with a saucer or plate and put a heavy weight on top. Refrigerate overnight. Turn out onto a serving dish, pour over any juices that have overflowed, and serve with whipped cream.

MICHAELMAS
· · · · · · · · · · · · · ·

IN Sussex, as elsewhere, rents fall due on Michaelmas Day, September 29. In earlier days tenants kept in their landlords' good graces by giving them a goose when they paid their rents. These birds are in prime condition at this time of the year, having been fattened on the gleanings from the harvest.

Roast goose

A 12 lb (5kg) goose
1½ tbs flour
1 pt (600 mls) stock from goose giblets

dry breadcrumbs
salt and black pepper

STUFF the goose (see recipe below), sprinkle it lightly with flour and roast in a pre-heated oven (200°C, gas 6) for 15 minutes. Reduce the heat to 160°C, gas 3 and continue cooking until the bird is tender, allowing about 25 minutes per pound weight, when stuffed. Remove fat several times during roasting. When goose is nearly done sprinkle the breast with the breadcrumbs and increase the heat to 200°C, gas 6 for the last 10-15 minutes of cooking. Remove to a serving dish and keep warm. Pour the fat from the roasting pan and add the flour to the remaining juices, stirring until the gravy thickens. Add stock, season, and strain into a gravy boat.

4 onions, peeled
1 oz (25g) butter
1 tsp dried sage or 12 chopped fresh sage leaves

4 ozs (100g) breadcrumbs
1 egg, beaten
1 tsp milk
salt and black pepper

Sage and onion stuffing

PUT the onions into a pan of boiling salted water and cook for 30 minutes until tender. Strain, cool and chop them up and then cook in the butter for 10 minutes. Cool again, and put into a bowl with the rest of the ingredients and mix well. Salt the cavity of the bird and fill with stuffing.

Apple sauce

2 lbs (900g) cooking apples,
peeled, cored and sliced

½ oz (14g) butter
2 tsp sugar

PUT the apples in a pan with a little water, cover and cook until they are soft. Mash them with a fork and add the butter and sugar, stirring well. Transfer to a bowl and serve hot.

OCTOBER
· · · · · · · ·

BATTLE OF Hastings 1066 is the date every schoolchild knows. But how many now the exact day and the month? It was on October 14 that the Normans led by Duke William met the Saxons, headed by Harold, on the slopes above the Senlac stream at what is now Battle.

Pheasant shooting has started. There is nothing to beat a roast pheasant with game chips, breadcrumbs, bread sauce and bacon rolls, but next month I have included an alternative recipe for this delicious bird. Winter vegetables are with us and can form the basis of some nourishing broths to warm the children after their Hallowe'en tricking and treating.

MENUS FOR THE MONTH		
First courses	**Main dishes**	**Puddings**
Cream of onion soup	Brewer's roast	Pears with crushed caramel
Smoked salmon pate	Braised steak with peppercorn sauce	Banana snow
Stuffed green peppers	Fish steaks with bacon	Iced pineapple with orange syrup
Melon with Selsey lobster	Duck and celery casserole	Boiled apple pudding

First courses

Cream of onion soup

2 medium onions, sliced thinly
2 ozs (50g) butter
1 tbs flour
1½ pts (900 mls) milk

salt and pepper
2 eggs
3 tbs double cream

MELT butter in a pan, add onion and cook until soft. Stir in flour. Bring milk to the boil, add slowly to the onion mixture, season and simmer for 10 minutes. Break eggs into a bowl, mix with the cream and beat well. Add to the onion mixture, adjust the seasoning to taste and serve with fried croutons.

Smoked salmon pate

4 ozs 100g) smoked salmon pieces
4 ozs (100g) curd cheese
2 tbs double cream
1 tbs grated onion
juice of half a lemon

dash of tabasco sauce
freshly ground black pepper
dill fronds, smoked salmon knots
and lemon triangles for decoration

ROUGHLY chop the smoked salmon and put in a food processor and blend until very fine. Add curd cheese and blend again until it is thoroughly mixed and an even coral pink colour. Add cream and blend to soften the texture, without losing the consistency. Stir in grated onion, lemon juice and tabasco and blend again for 10 seconds. Season with generous amount of black pepper. Transfer to a serving dish and decorate the top with the dill fronds, smoked salmon knots and lemon triangles.

Stuffed green peppers

4 large, firm peppers
4 ozs (100g) rice
2 cloves of garlic, crushed
8 ozs (225g) cooked minced pork
1 onion, minced and sauted in butter

1 egg
salt and pepper
paprika
tomato sauce

BOIL the rice. Cut peppers near to the stalk and remove seeds and inner ribs. Mix the minced pork with the garlic and onion, add the beaten egg, cooked rice, salt and pepper. Mix well and put into the peppers. Stand them in an ovenproof dish, pour tomato sauce (see recipe on page 92) over them and bake in a moderate oven (180°C, gas 4) until the peppers are tender. Baste several times during cooking. Serve hot or cold.

Melon with Selsey lobster

1 cooked lobster
1 Galia or Cantaloupe melon
1/4 pt (150 mls) single cream

1/2 pt (300 mls) mayonnaise
1/2 small tin tomato puree
pinch paprika

SHELL the lobster, clean and cut the meat into cubes. Cut the top off the melon and remove the pips from inside the centre. Using a melon baller scoop out the flesh into balls and place in a bowl with the lobster cubes. Mix the mayonnaise with cream and tomato puree and season with paprika. Combine with the melon and lobster and place in the fridge to chill. When cold spoon the mixture into the hollowed-out melon or serve in individual dishes, decorated with sprigs of parsley.

Main dishes

Brewer's roast
(Leg of lamb in gin)

leg of lamb weighing not more
than 5 lbs (2.2kg), boned
8 fl ozs gin

4 ozs (100g) juniper berries
coarse salt and black pepper
4-6 ozs (100-175g) unsalted butter

SOAK the juniper berries overnight in half the gin, sealing the glass to prevent evaporation. On the morning before the lamb is to be cooked, flatten it and season the cut side generously with the salt, pepper and half the butter. Drain the berries and spread them over the seasoned lamb. Roll the joint up and sew the leg together with a large eyed curved needle and string. Refrigerate until needed, then spread the rest of the butter over the meat and season again with salt and pepper. Place on a rack in a roasting pan and cook in a moderate oven (180°C, gas 4) for 20 minutes per pound and 20 minutes over, basting with its own juices. Remove from oven and allow to rest for 10 to 15 minutes, then heat the rest of the gin, pour it over the joint and set light to it. When the flames die down carve and serve with vegetables of your choice.

Braised steak with green
peppercorn sauce
(serves two)

1lb (450g) braising steak
1 large onion, peeled and sliced
1 tbs beef dripping
4 fl ozs dry white wine or cider
3 tsp green peppercorns

1 tsp tomato puree
1 heaped tsp flour
1 clove garlic
1 sprig thyme
salt and black pepper

MELT dripping in a pan and put in the steak. Fry until sealed on both sides, then remove and transfer to a casserole. Add the onion to the fat in the pan and fry until brown. Spread the browned onion over the meat. Tilt off any excess fat and add the wine (or vinegar) to the remaining juices, stir well and simmer. Pour over the meat and onions and add the thyme, crushed garlic and seasoning. Cover casserole and braise in a moderate oven (160°C, gas 3) for two hours. Transfer the meat and onions to a serving dish and keep warm. Pour off the remaining liquid from the casserole into a liquidiser. Add the flour, tomato puree and two teaspoonfuls of the green peppercorns. Blend, then pour into a saucepan with the remaining peppercorns. Bring to simmering point and pour over the meat.

Baked fish steaks with bacon

4 steaks of white fish
2 carrots, thinly sliced
1 stick celery, thinly sliced
4 ozs (100g) mushrooms, thinly sliced
4 slices back bacon
1 large onion, thinly sliced

2 tbs chopped parsley
1/2 tsp dried thyme
4 slices lemon
2 ozs (50g) butter
1/2 pt (300 mls) white wine
salt and black pepper

PRE-HEAT oven to 220°C, gas 7. Place the bacon slices on the bottom of a greased dish, cover them with the carrots, mushrooms, celery, and onion and pour in the wine. Cover tightly with foil and bake for 30 minutes. Remove dish from the oven and arrange the fish steaks on top of the vegetables. Sprinkle with parsley, thyme, salt and pepper and place a lemon slice on each steak. Dot with butter. Cover the dish again and bake for a further 20 minutes in a moderate oven (180°C, gas 4). Serve with potatoes mashed with sour cream and flavoured with nutmeg.

Duck and celery casserole

4 lb (1.8kg) duck cut into four
portions, washed and dried
1 medium onion, peeled and chopped
3 rashers lean bacon, chopped
1 oz (25g) butter

1 level tbs flour
1/2 pt (300 mls) chicken stock
salt and fresh ground pepper
1/4 level tsp mixed herbs
1 small head celery

CUT away excess fat from duck portions and put them in a large casserole. Fry onion and bacon gently in butter until pale gold. Stir in flour, cook for two minutes and then gradually blend in the stock. Cook, stirring, until sauce comes to the boil and thickens. Reduce heat and season to taste with salt and pepper. Stir in the herbs and then pour the sauce over the duck. Cut the celery into one inch lengths and add to the casserole. Cover with a lid or kitchen foil. Cook in the centre of a moderate oven (180°C, gas 4) for about one and a half to two hours, until the duck is tender.

• •

Puddings

Poached pears with crushed caramel

4 ripe pears, peeled
1 wineglass sweet white wine
cold water to cover
1 tbs castor sugar
squeeze lemon juice

3 tbs Demerara sugar
For the caramel:
¼ pt (150mls) water
4 oz (100g) castor sugar

PLACE whole peeled pears in a saucepan. Pour over the wine and sufficient water to cover. Add the castor sugar and lemon juice and poach
pears gently until tender. Remove from pan with a draining spoon and
keep on a plate to one side. Pour the poaching juices into a clean pan and
add the Demerara sugar. Bring to boil and bubble to reduce until syrupy.
Put on one side.

To make the caramel: Dissolve the water and castor sugar in a
saucepan and then boil until golden and caramelised. Pour into a shallow, lightly oiled, baking tray and leave to set. When set, break up with a
meat tenderising hammer or rolling pin. Put pears into individual bowls
or sweet dishes and pour syrupy juice over each. Sprinkle the tops with
crushed caramel. Serve with double cream.

Banana snow

6 medium-sized bananas, peeled
  and mashed to a puree
3 tbs lemon juice
2 cartons natural or banana yoghurt
4 level tbs castor sugar

¼ pt (150 mls) double cream
2 egg whites
1 oz (25g) grated plain
  chocolate for decoration

MASH the bananas with the lemon juice to a puree. Stir in the yoghurt
and sugar and mix well. Whip cream until fairly stiff and beat the egg
whites into stiff peaks. Fold cream and egg whites into banana mixture.
Pile into individual bowls or glass dishes and refrigerate until needed.
Before serving scatter grated chocolate over the top of each portion.

EGG TIP: If egg whites will not whisk it is probably
because they have come straight from the fridge. Better
to use ones that have been at room temperature.

Iced pineapple
with orange syrup

10 ozs (275g) fresh or tinned
pineapple rings
8 ozs (225g) sugar
4 thin-skinned oranges, un-peeled and
cut into quarter inch slices

8 fl ozs water
1 oz (25g) toasted, flaked almonds
2 tbs orange-flavoured liqueur
1 tbs brandy

ARRANGE the pineapple rings in a shallow serving dish. In a large saucepan, dissolve the sugar in the water over a moderate heat, stirring constantly with a wooden spoon. When dissolved, bring the syrup to the boil and add the orange slices, overlapping them so that they are covered by the syrup. Reduce the heat to low and simmer the oranges for 20 minutes, or until the pith and skin are tender when pierced with a knife. Remove from the syrup with a draining spoon and lay slices neatly over the pineapple rings. Increase the heat to moderately high and boil the syrup for 10 to 15 minutes, or until it turns a pale golden brown colour. Remove the pan from the heat, stir in the almonds and pour the syrup over the fruit. Leave to cool slightly. Place the dish in the fridge to chill for at least one hour. Sprinkle the fruit with the orange-flavoured liqueur and the brandy and serve.

Boiled apple pudding

For the suet crust:
8 ozs plain flour
2 level tsp baking powder
4 ozs suet, finely shredded
water to mix
pinch of salt

For the filling:
1fi lbs (675g) apples, peeled,
cored and sliced
sugar to taste
water
custard or cream to finish

SIEVE flour, salt and baking powder into a bowl. Add the suet and mix to a paste with cold water. Roll out thinly and line a large, greased pudding basin with the dough. Keep some to make a lid. Put the apples into the lined basin, sprinkle with sugar and add enough water to half cover the fruit. Roll out the remaining dough to make the lid, damp the edges and put on top the pudding, pressing the edges to seal them. Cover with a double thickness of greaseproof paper, tied on with string, or a double thickness of foil. Boil for two hours, or, for a lighter pudding, steam over boiling water for two and a half to three hours. Serve with custard or with cream.

N•OVEMBER

BONFIRE NIGHT has been celebrated seriously in Sussex for nearly 400 years. Traditionally everyone eats bonfire-baked potatoes and hot sausages but suggestions for other nosh for noisy nights are given on pages 77 to 82. Guy Fawkes apart, this is a good month for foodies. Root vegetables are in plentiful supply and beef and pork at their best. There is also a great variety of white fish available and plenty of game.

MENUS FOR THE MONTH		
First courses	**Main dishes**	**Puddings**
French onion soup	Salmi of pheasant	Gingernut pudding
Anchovy eggs	Cod steaks in cider	Caramel cream
Smoked mackerel	Chicken paprika	Lemon surprise
mousse	Carbonnade	Chestnut
Soft roe pate	of beef	meringue

First courses

French onion soup

4 ozs (100g) Gruyere cheese, sliced
3 lbs (1.2kg) onions, peeled
and finely sliced
2 ozs (50g) butter
1 tbs oil
salt

2 grindings black pepper
1½ ozs (40g) flour
2 pts (1.2 ls) beef stock, from cube
¼ pt (150 mls) white wine
¾ tsp sugar
4 slices French bread

MELT butter and oil in a large saucepan, add the onions and cook until golden. Add salt, pepper and sugar. Add the flour and blend thoroughly. Simmer for half an hour. Make the beef stock from the cube and pour it, while still hot, with the wine, into the saucepan. Put on the lid and continue cooking for a further ten minutes. Cover each slice of French bread with a slice of Gruyere cheese. Just before serving float a piece of cheese-covered bread on the surface of each bowl of soup and place under a hot grill until the cheese bubbles.

Anchovy eggs

4 hard-boiled eggs, shelled
1 tsp anchovy essence
1 tbs mayonnaise

For decoration:
2 anchovies, halved and rolled up
8 lettuce leaves, washed and dried

WHEN cool cut the tips off both ends of the eggs and set aside. Halve each egg through the middle and turn out the yolks into a basin and chop them up. Add the anchovy essence and the mayonnaise and mix well together. Put two leaves of lettuce into each bowl or glass dish and place two eggs halves on them. Fill the eggs with the anchovy and mayonnaise mixture and cap each one with the end pieces and a rolled half anchovy.

Smoked mackerel mousse

3 large smoked mackerel fillets
6 ozs (175g) double cream
1/4 pt (150 mls) mayonnaise
1 tbs brandy
1 tbs grated horseradish
1/2 clove garlic
1 shallot, finely chopped

1/2 oz (14g) powdered gelatine
salt and pepper
lemon juice
vegetable oil
sliced cucumber, sliced lemon and chives for garnish

SKIN mackerel fillets and remove any bones. Mix lemon juice with enough hot water to make three tablespoonfuls, add the gelatine and heat gently to melt. Put fillets into food processor with the brandy, mayonnaise, salt, pepper, garlic and chopped shallot. Work until smooth then, with the machine still running, pour in the gelatine. Transfer mixture to a bowl and refrigerate until it begins to thicken. Lightly whip the cream and fold into the mousse, then pour the mixture into a mould lightly smeared with vegetable oil. Chill in fridge overnight, or until set. Turn out on to serving plate and garnish with sliced cucumber, lemon and chives.

Soft roe pate

4 ozs (100g) butter
6 ozs (175g) soft roes
salt
8 grindings black pepper

grated rind and juice of half a lemon
2 tbs chopped parsley
1 tbs chopped parsley for garnish

FRY the seasoned roes gently in one ounce of the butter for about five minutes, turning them once or twice. Put into a liquidiser with lemon juice, parsley and remainder of melted butter and blend until smooth. Transfer to individual dishes or one serving dish. Refrigerate and then garnish with a mixture of finely grated lemon peel and parsley.

Main dishes

Salmi of pheasant

1 pheasant, plucked, drawn and trussed
4 rashers streaky bacon
3-4 tbs port
2 tsps redcurrant jelly
6 ozs (175g) button mushrooms, washed and dried
2 slices bread
butter
For the sauce:
1 oz (25g) butter
1 tsp olive oil
1 oz lean ham or bacon, chopped

½ small peeled onion, chopped
½ small celery stalk, chopped
1 oz (25g) mushrooms and stalks, chopped
½ small carrot, peeled and sliced
1 oz (25g) flour
¾ pt (450 mls) beef stock, from cube
2 level tsps tomato puree
1 small bay leaf
2 sprigs parsley
salt and pepper

PUT butter and oil into a pan and heat until both are sizzling. Add the ham or bacon, onion, celery, mushrooms and carrot. Fry gently for about 10 minutes until golden brown. Add the flour and cook, stirring constantly, until it turns light brown. Gradually blend in the stock, continue to stir until the sauce comes to the boil and thickens. Add tomato puree, bay leaf and parsley. Cover pan and simmer gently for 30 minutes. Strain and season to taste with salt and pepper.

Prepare the pheasant for roasting by covering breast with four rashers of streaky bacon. Roast for 20 minutes in a moderately hot oven (200°C, gas 6). Remove from oven and take off bacon rashers, then cut the pheasant into neat joints and remove the skin. Place the bird in a fairly large flameproof casserole and add three quarters of a pint of the sauce, redcurrant jelly and port. Cover and simmer very gently for 30 minutes. Add the mushrooms and continue to simmer for a further 10 to 15 minutes, or until the bird is tender. Cut each slice of bread into four triangles and fry gently in butter until crisp and golden. Uncover casserole and stand triangles of fried bread round the edge of the dish before serving

TEMPERATURE TIP: For deep frying the temperature should be 180°C - 190°C. If you do not have a thermometer drop a cube of bread into the hot fat and if it browns in one minute the temperature is right.

Cod steaks in cider

4 cod steaks
1 oz (25g) butter
1 medium onion, thinly sliced

1 carrot, scraped and sliced
½ pt (300 mls) dry cider
chopped parsley for garnish

MELT the butter in a large saucepan over moderate heat. When the foam subsides add the onion and carrot. Cook, stirring occasionally, until the onion is soft and the carrot thoroughly cooked. Pour in the cider and bring to the boil. Reduce the heat, then add the cod steaks to the pan. Poach slowly until the flesh flakes easily when tested with a fork. Have a warmed, buttered serving dish ready and put in the steaks, covering them liberally with the sauce and some chopped parsley.

Chicken paprika

4 portions chicken
2 medium onions, chopped
1 green pepper, de-seeded
and cut into small strips
1 small tin chopped tomatoes
¼ pt (150 mls) chicken stock, from cube

1 dsp flour
1 heaped tbs paprika
5 oz (150g) carton soured cream
oil for cooking
salt and black pepper
2 good pinches cayenne

PRE-HEAT oven to 160°C gas 3. Heat a little oil in a frying pan and fry chicken until nicely browned. Transfer, using a draining spoon, to a casserole and season. In the oil left in the pan, fry onions until soft. Stir in the flour, cayenne and paprika to soak up all the juices. Add tomatoes and stir them around and then add the stock. Bring to simmering point and pour over the chicken. Cover and bake for 45 minutes. Stir in the chopped pepper, replace the lid and cook for a further 30 minutes. Just before serving spoon the soured cream on the top and mix it to give a marbled effect. Sprinkle over a dusting of paprika.

Carbonnade
of beef

2 lbs (900g) stewing steak
½ pt (300mls) brown ale or Guinness
2 large onions, peeled and sliced
2 cloves of garlic peeled and crushed

1 oz (25g) of butter
1 tbs tomato puree
1 tbs flour
salt and ground black pepper

CUT the beef into cubes and put into a casserole with the beer and cook in a medium hot oven (190°C, gas 5) for about two hours, stirring occasionally. Meantime cook the onions slowly in a pan with the crushed garlic. When they become transparent add the tomato puree. Take the casserole out of the oven, add the flour to the meat and beer and then add the onions, garlic and bouquet garni. Put the dish back in the oven for about 15 minutes and when ready to serve, remove the bouquet garni, transfer to a serving dish and scatter triangles of fried bread and the parsley over the top and serve with boiled or mashed potatoes and a green vegetables.

Puddings

Gingernut pudding ✳ *EXCELLENT*

8 ozs (225g) packet of gingernuts
½ pt (300 mls) double cream

1 tsp castor sugar
1 small can mandarin oranges, drained

THIS pudding should be made the day before it is to be eaten.
Lightly whip the cream then slightly sweeten it with the sugar. Take a small round serving dish and place a layer of broken ginger nuts on the bottom. Cover with a layer of mandarins, followed by a thin layer of whipped cream. Repeat this layering until all the ingredients have been used, finishing with a layer of whipped cream. Cover the serving dish with a lid or foil and leave in the fridge overnight.

Caramel cream

For the caramel
6 ozs (175g) castor sugar
2 tbs water
For the custard:
2 whole eggs

2 egg yolks
2 ozs (50g) castor sugar
½ pt (300 mls) milk
½ pt (300 mls) single cream
few drops vanilla essence

PUT the sugar and water into a small thick-bottomed saucepan and allow it to dissolve over a low heat, without stirring. When dissolved turn up the heat and begin stirring. Continue to cook until it becomes a good caramel brown. Take it off the heat and pour it into a warm circular glass dish or ring. Pre-heat oven to 160°C, gas 3. Mix eggs, egg yolks and sugar in a bowl. Heat the milk and cream, but do not boil. Pour into the eggs and add a few drops of vanilla essence. Stir well, then pour into the glass dish on top of the caramel. Stand the dish in a roasting pan of cold water. Cover with greaseproof paper and bake for one hour, until set. Leave to get cold. Cover the glass dish or ring with an inverted plate and turn upside down, so it is turned out with the caramel on top.

Lemon surprise

3 eggs, separated
juice and grated rind of 1 lemon

8 ozs (225g) castor sugar
8 fl ozs double cream

TURN the thermostat of the fridge to its coldest setting. In a small bowl beat together the egg yolks and lemon juice and rind with a metal spoon. Set aside. In a medium-sized mixing bowl, beat the egg whites until they are stiff. Beat in the sugar, a little at a time, and continue beating until the mixture forms stiff peaks. In a large bowl, beat the cream until it is stiff. Using a metal spoon, carefully fold the egg whites into the cream and then fold in the egg yolks. Spoon the mixture into a two pint pudding basin. Place the basin in the frozen food compartment of the fridge and freeze the mixture for one to one and a half hours, or until it is completely set. Turn out of the basin 10 minutes before serving and divide into individual serving bowls.

Chestnut meringue

For meringue:
4 egg whites
8 ozs (225g) castor sugar
for filling:
1 lb (450g) chestnuts
1 vanilla pod
2 tbs sugar

4 tbs water
¼ pt (150 mls) double
cream, whipped
for decoration:
icing sugar
1 oz (25g) plain chocolate, grated

PRE-HEAT oven to 140°C, gas 1. Line two baking sheets with non stick kitchen paper. Whisk egg whites in a bowl until stiff. Add one table-spoonful of the sugar and whisk for a minute. Fold in the rest of the sugar with a metal spoon. Divide mixture evenly between the two trays and spread carefully in two rounds, eight or nine inches in diameter. For a more professional appearance use a nylon forcing bag fitted with a half inch eclair nozzle and pipe meringue to form a circle, starting from the centre. Bake in the pre-heated oven for about an hour, until lightly coloured and quite dry. Put on a wire tray, peel off the paper and leave to cool. Meanwhile skin and cook the chestnuts with a vanilla pod for added flavour, transfer to a liquidiser and blend to a puree. Dissolve sugar in water in a pan, bring to the boil and pour carefully into a small bowl or cup. Leave to cool. Blend this sugar syrup into the chestnut puree. Whip the cream and add half of it to the puree. Use this mixture to sandwich together the two rounds of meringue. Dust the top with icing sugar, and decorate with the remaining cream and the grated chocolate.

BONFIRE
·········

ON Guy Fawkes Night you may well be required to feed the famished from 5pm to 5am so there has to be plenty of food, and a good variety of it. People who are keen on processions and pyrotechnics develop a keen appetite – it is all that walking about. In Lewes they are particularly peripatetic, moving from house to house, having a sausage here, some soup there. Numbers can vary from a couple of friends to a houseful, so catering has to be flexible.

It is processions and pedestrians only in the centre of Lewes from 5pm, and any time after that the parties start. First needing to be fed are the out-of-towners who have come in early, gratefully accepting your kind offer of somewhere to settle while waiting for the fun to begin. Tea, sandwiches (see January) and cake should keep them happy, with one or two little extras such as eggs in an overcoat, smoked salmon rolls or ham and cheese cornets to add an interest.

Have the soup or soups on the heat from 7pm onwards. The biggest eat is around 8pm. The grand procession ends about then and the societies take a breather, and some refreshment, before moving off to their respective bonfire sites.

All the recipes are for four, so simply double, treble or quadruple the quantities of ingredients as you need to. Do as much shopping and preparation as you can well in advance. Some of these dishes, and all of the soups, can be made the day before, and refrigerated.

Finger food	Soups	Filling finger food
Hot sausage savouries	Creole soup	Chicken vol au vents
Smoked salmon rolls	Pepper pot soup	Herb and sausage patties
Eggs in overcoats	Sauerkraut and	
Ham and cottage	sausage soup	Jacket potatoes
cheese cornets	Fish soup	Sausage plait

Finger food

Hot sausage
savouries

8 ozs (225g) skinless pork sausages or
sausage meat
1 large egg
2 tsps milk

1½ ozs (40g) toasted breadcrumbs
2 level tsps dry mustard
½ level tsp salt
fat or oil for frying.

CUT each sausage into four pieces. Beat egg and milk well together. Combine breadcrumbs, mustard and salt. Coat pieces of sausage with egg and milk mixture. Toss in breadcrumb mixture and be sure it sticks well. Fry in hot fat or oil until crisp and golden. Remove from pan, drain well on kitchen paper and serve hot.

Smoked salmon
rolls

4 ozs (100g) smoked salmon slices.
small jar of lumpfish roe,
4 ozs (100g) Philadelphia

cream cheese
1 tsp lemon juice
1 grinding of black pepper.

Mix all the ingredients together, except the smoked salmon. Divide the mixture into four sausage-shaped rolls and place on the smoked salmon. Roll up, secure with cocktail sticks if necessary, and serve on lettuce leaves with lemon wedges and brown bread and butter.

Eggs in their
overcoats

4 hard boiled eggs
1 lb (450g) pork sausage meat
1 medium sized onion, finely chopped

4 tbs peanut butter
1 clove garlic, crushed,
2 ozs (50g) fresh breadcrumbs,

MIX the sausage meat, onion, garlic, peanut butter and breadcrumbs together in a bowl. Divide into four and put a cold peeled egg in the middle of each portion. Enclose the egg completely with the mixture. Brush each wrapped egg with oil and put on a greased baking tray. Pre-heat the oven to 200°C, gas 6 and cook for half an hour, or until nicely brown. Leave to cool before serving.

Ham and cottage cheese cornets

8 ozs (225g) cottage cheese
8 ozs (225g) tin of pineapple pieces
4 slices cooked ham
1 small red pepper, cored,

seeded and finely chopped
1 stick of celery, diced
lettuce or cress for decoration

MIX all the ingredients together thoroughly, except the ham. Divide the filling between the slices of ham and roll each one up in a cornet shape and arrange on a bed of lettuce or cress on a serving dish.

Soups

Creole soup

1 tbs chopped green pepper
1 tbs chopped onion
2 tbs butter
2 tbs flour
1 pt (600 mls) beef stock from a cube
or 1 pt (600 mls) canned consomme

salt and pepper
pinch of cayenne
1 tbs horseradish sauce
2 tbs macaroni pieces, cooked
7 oz (200g) tin tomatoes with juice

COOK peppers and onions in butter for five minutes. Add flour, mix well, then add the stock and tomatoes. Simmer for 15 minutes. Strain and season with salt, pepper and cayenne. Just before serving add the horseradish and pieces of macaroni.

Pepper pot soup

1 onion, finely chopped
2 sticks celery, finely chopped
half green pepper finely chopped
2 tbs butter
1 tbs flour

2 pts (1.2 ls) chicken stock
made with two cubes
6 grindings of black pepper
3 ozs (75g) cold cubed potatoes
1/4 pt (150 mls) double cream

FRY the onions, celery, green pepper and potatoes gently in butter for about 15 minutes. Add the flour and stir well. Pour in a little of the stock and season. Transfer the mixture to a large saucepan, pour in the remaining stock, stir well, cover and simmer for half an hour or until the vegetables are really tender. Put into a liquidiser and blend for about a minute. When serving add a spoonful of cream to each portion.

Sauerkraut and sausage soup

1 oz (25g) butter
1 tbs paprika
1 tbs flour
2½ pts (1.5 ls) water
salt and ½ tsp ground black pepper

jar or can af sauerkraut, drained.
8 slices garlic sausage
5 fl ozs sour cream.

MELT the butter in a large saucepan and stir in the paprika and flour. Stir thoroughly for two to three minutes and then add the water and bring to the boil, stirring constantly. Add the sauerkraut and sausage. Season. Cover pan and simmer for half an hour. Pour into bowls and add some sour cream to each serving.

Fish chowder

2 large potatoes, peeled and diced
2 large onions, peeled and diced
1 small swede, finely chopped
1 small piece celeriac, finely chopped
½ clove garlic, crushed
1 stick celery, finely chopped
10 ozs (275g) white fish,
skinned and diced

pinch of mixed herbs
good pinch celery salt
1 bay leaf
1¾ pts (1 litre) chicken stock,
made from cubes
¼ pt (150 mls) cream
chopped watercress, grated cheese
and paprika for garnish

PUT all the vegetables into a casserole with the seasoning, bay leaf and stock. Cover and cook in a slow oven (150°C, gas 2) for 45 minutes. Remove and add the raw fish. Return to the oven and continue cooking for a half an hour. Stir in the cream before serving, garnished with the watercress and sprinkled with grated cheese and paprika.

Filling finger food

Chicken and mushroom vol au vents

4 frozen or home made vol au vents cases
4 ozs (100g) cooked chicken
2 ozs (50g) mushrooms, washed,
dried and chopped

½ oz (14g) butter
¼ pt (150 mls) white sauce
2 tsps lemon juice

PUT the vol au vent cases on a baking tray, brush the tops with a little milk and bake in a hot oven (220°C, gas 7) for 20 minutes until crisp and golden. Remove from oven and lift off the lids. Cut chicken into small pieces. Lightly fry the mushrooms in butter. Make the white sauce (see recipe on page 93) and then add to it the chicken, mushrooms, lemon juice and any seasoning you think necessary. Stir well, allow to cool, and then spoon equal amounts of the filling into the pastry cases and put the lids back on. Ten minutes before you want to serve the vol au vents put them into a pre-heated oven at 160°C, gas 3, to heat up.

Herb and sausage patties

1 lb (450g) pork sausage meat
1 tsp dried mixed herbs
1 tbs Worcestershire Sauce
3 grindings black pepper

oil for frying.
4 baps or soft rolls
butter
prepared English mustard

MIX together the sausage meat, herbs, Worcester sauce and pepper Form the mixture into four patties. Heat the oil and fry the patties for three or four minutes on one side and then turn them and fry for a further three or four minutes on the other side. Split the baps or rolls in half and spread with butter and a little mustard and then put a patty between the two halves.

Jacket potatoes

4 large baking potatoes
salad oil
1 oz (25g) butter
4 tbs milk

level tsp of made mustard
4 ozs (100g) grated Cheddar cheese or
6 ozs (175g) fried bacon, diced
salt and pepper

SCRUB and dry potatoes. Prick all over with a fork. Brush with salad oil and stand on a baking tray in oven. Bake at 190°C, gas 5 for one and a half to two hours. When cool enough to handle cut each in half lengthways. Spoon insides into a bowl with butter, milk and mustard, then add grated cheese or fried bacon. Mix well with the potato, season and return mixture to potato cases. Leave until ten minutes before required and then put in a hot oven (220°C, gas 7) for 10 to fifteen minutes.

BONFIRE NIGHT BUMPER: Pour a bottle of full bodied red wine into a saucepan, add a large apple spiked with with cloves, and heat gently for about five minutes, but do not allow to boil. Add hot water to achieve the strength you want and ladle into warmed glasses. Cheers.

Sausage plait

8ozs (225g) short crust pastry
1lb (450g) pork sausage meat
4 ozs (100g) mushrooms,
cleaned and sliced
1 onion, peeled a finely chopped

2 tbs chopped parsley
1 egg, beaten
grated Parmesan cheese
salt and black pepper
milk

ROLL out the pastry to a rectangle measuring about 10 inches by eight inches, saving the trimmings. Put the sausage meat, chopped onions and mushrooms in a bowl and mix together with the beaten egg. Add the chopped parsley and season. Place the mixture in the centre of the pastry rectangle, draw up the sides, moisten the overlap with milk and seal. Trim the ends of the pastry roll, fold them up and also moisten and seal. With a sharp knife score divisions across the top of the pastry, about three quarters of an inch wide. Roll out the trimmings and cut three half inch wide strips; plait them together and place on the top of the roll. Brush with the milk and sprinkle with grated Parmesan. Put on a greased and floured baking tray and cook in a pre-heated moderate oven (180°C, gas 4) for half an hour, or until the pastry is golden brown. Remove from the oven and place on a wire rack to cool, or serve hot.

• •

DECEMBER
D · · · · · · · · · · ·

MOST people have their own favourite foods and recipes for Christmas, turkey featuring largely among them, so I have only included one recipe to help use up that seemingly endless supply of cold bird. Mincemeat is featured in two rather novel ways – in a suet pudding with apples and in an ice cream. Sussex appetites were extremely robust in earlier days. At Ockenden Manor, Cuckfield in 1702 Timothy Burrell's Christmas guests were offered 15 courses every time they dined. The menus are all in his journal.

MENUS FOR THE MONTH

First courses	Main dishes	Puddings
Tuna and bean vinaigrette	Turkey pasta	Mincemeat and apple pudding
Cream cheese consomme	Chicken with French mustard	Tangerine cream
Brussels sprout soup	Corn and haddock bake	Christmas pudding ice cream
Spicy prawns mayonnaise	Pork steaks Provencale	Quick party trifle

First courses

Tuna and bean vinaigrette

8 ozs (225g) tin butter beans, drained
8 ozs (225g) tin tuna fish in oil, drained and flaked
1 small shallot, peeled and chopped

1 tbs parsley, finely chopped
extra chopped parsley for garnish
salt and pepper
vinaigrette, see recipe on page 93

PLACE drained beans in a bowl with the onion, parsley, tuna, salt and pepper. Pour vinaigrette over the bean mixture, and stir in with wooden spoon making sure it is all well covered. Transfer to a serving dish, spreading evenly around the surface. Arrange the tuna fish on top. Sprinkle with fresh olive oil and chopped parsley.

Cream cheese consomme

10 fl oz can consomme	1 tbs chopped chives
3 ozs (75g) Philadelphia cream cheese	¼ oz (7g) pkt gelatine

HEAT consomme, put aside four tablespoonfuls, and whisk the gelatine into the remainder until thoroughly dissolved. Cut the cheese into pieces and put in a bowl, pour in the hot consomme and whisk together until smooth and creamy. Pour into individual ramekins and put in the fridge to set. When really firm pour a tablespoonful of the reserved consomme over the top of each ramekin and but them back into the fridge until ready to serve, garnished with chopped chives.

Brussels sprout soup
with croutons

8 ozs (225g) sprouts, trimmed	1 oz (25g) butter
and well washed	½ pt (300 mls) milk
1 medium onion, peeled and cut up	¼ pt (150 mls) double cream
2 ozs (50g) chopped ham	croutons
1½ pts (900 mls) chicken stock	salt and pepper
1 oz (25g) flour	

DROP the sprouts into boiling salted water and cook until they are tender but still firm. Drain and cut up. Put the butter in a pan, add the onion and ham and sweat over a low heat for 10 minutes. Add the sprouts and stock and simmer gently for half an hour and then put into a liquidiser and blend for only a minute to mix everything together. Return soup to the pan and thicken with the flour mixed with the milk. When serving, pour a little cream into each portion, followed by a spoonful of hot croutons.

Spicy prawn
mayonnaise

6 ozs (175g) prawns, peeled	¼ pt mayonnaise
2 hard boiled eggs, quartered	½ tsp chilli sauce
4 small tomatoes, peeled and quartered	chopped parsley to garnish
½ green pepper, cut into small squares	

PREPARE the prawns, eggs, tomatoes and pepper and put into individual dishes. Mix the mayonnaise and chilli sauce well together and pour over each portion. Refrigerate until ready to serve, then garnish with the chopped parsley.

Main dishes

Turkey pasta
(serves eight)

1 lb (450g) cooked turkey,
cut into small pieces
8 ozs (225g) spaghetti, broken
into short lengths
4 ozs (100g) button mushrooms,
washed, dried and sliced
2 onions, peeled and sliced thinly
salt and freshly ground black pepper

For the sauce:
2 ozs (50g) butter
2 ozs (50g) flour
1 pt (600 mls) chicken stock, from cube
¼ pt (150 mls) whipping cream
wine glass sherry
2 ozs (50g) flaked almonds
2 ozs (50g) Cheddar cheese, grated

BOIL and drain the spaghetti and spread it over the bottom of an oven-proof serving dish. Heat the butter in a frying pan and saute the onions and mushrooms. Add flour, mix in well, and gradually stir in the stock. Bring to the boil and when it has thickened remove from heat and add the cream and sherry, stirring well. Season to taste and add the turkey pieces. Pour the mixture on to the spaghetti and cover with the grated cheese. Sprinkle over the almonds and bake in a moderately hot oven (190°C, gas 5) for 30 minutes, or until golden brown.

Chicken with French mustard

1 medium chicken, quartered
small jar Dijon mustard
3 ozs (75g) butter
salt and pepper
glass dry white wine
good pinch mixed herbs

3 cloves garlic, crushed
¼ pt (150 mls) chicken
stock, from a cube
8 baby onions
8 small carrots
8 artichoke hearts, bottled in oil

MELT butter in a flameproof casserole and brown the chicken pieces in it. Add the salt, pepper, wine, herbs, garlic and chicken stock and stir gently to mix together. Cook for 35 minutes in a moderate oven (180°C, gas 4). Remove from oven, add the onions, carrots, artichoke hearts and simmer over a moderate heat for ten minutes. Using a draining spoon, transfer the chicken and vegetables from the casserole to a heated serving dish and keep warm. Stir the Dijon mustard into the liquid in which the chicken has been cooked. Bring to the boil and then reduce the heat and add the flour. Simmer to thicken. Cover the chicken and vegetables with the sauce and keep hot until ready to serve.

Corn and haddock bake

1lb (450g) smoked haddock	*1 oz (25g) flour*
8 fl ozs milk	*salt and pepper*
large can of sweetcorn	*4 tbs grated strong cheese*
2 ozs (50g) butter	*4 tomatoes, halved*
a little extra butter	*parsley for garnish*

POACH the haddock gently in milk, drain and flake the fish, reserving the milk. Remove skin and bones and place in a greased ovenproof dish. Drain the tin of sweetcorn, keeping the liquid, and add the corn to the fish. Make a sauce with the butter, flour, fish liquid and sweet corn liquid. When it thickens season with salt and pepper and pour over the fish. Sprinkle with grated cheese and bake in a hot oven (200°C, gas 6) for about 20 minutes. Grill the tomato halves and place on top of the fish when it is cooked. Sprinkle all over with parsley.

Pork steaks Provencale

Four 5oz (150g) pork steaks	*1 clove garlic, crushed*
For the sauce:	*2 sticks celery, chopped*
1 dsp sunflower oil	*pinch marjoram*
8 ozs (225g) can chopped tomatoes	*salt and black pepper*
2 shallots, chopped	

BRUSH the steaks with a little oil and cook under a hot grill for about eight minutes each side. Meanwhile make the sauce. Heat the oil in a saucepan and add the shallots, garlic and celery. Saute for one minute. Drain the juice from the tomatoes and keep on one side. Add the chopped tomatoes to the onion mixture with the marjoram, salt and pepper and sufficient tomato juice to produce a thick sauce. Bring to the boil, reduce heat, and simmer for five to 10 minutes. Pour the sauce over the pork steaks and serve with vegetables of your choice.

• •

Puddings

Mincemeat and apple pudding

2 large Bramley apples	8 ozs (225g) self raising flour
10 ozs (275g) mincemeat	4 ozs (100g) shredded beef suet
2 tbs golden syrup	½ tsp salt
For suet crust:	4 fl ozs water

SIEVE the flour and salt together in a mixing bowl, add the suet and mix with the water until a paste is formed and the sides of the bowl are clean. Grate the apples roughly and mix with the mincemeat. Grease a two and a half pint pudding basin and put the syrup in the bottom. Roll the pastry out thinly and cut out four circles, one to cover the bottom of the basin, another to cover the top and two for the middle. Put the smallest circle in the bottom on top of the syrup and cover it with a layer of the mincemeat and apple mixture. Put another pastry circle on top followed by another layer of mincemeat until the basin has the fourth pastry circle on top. Cover the basin with a double layer of greased greaseproof paper or foil and steam for about two and a half hours. Turn out on to a dish and serve with cream.

Tangerine cream

3 tangerines, or clementines	1 rounded dsp gelatine
6-8 sugar lumps	5 tbs boiling water
¾ pt (450 mls) milk	1 egg white
1 tbs castor sugar	¼ pt (150 mls) double cream
3 egg yolks	2-3 tbs redcurrant jelly

RUB the sugar lumps over the rind of the washed tangerines or clementines to remove all the zest. When well soaked with the zest, put sugar lumps in a pan with the milk and dissolve over a gentle heat. Beat yolks well with sugar in a bowl. Pour in the milk, return to the pan and stir over the heat until it thickens. On no account let the milk boil. Strain and cool. Dissolve the gelatine in the boiling water. Whip the egg white and then the cream and mix together. Add the gelatine to the custard mixture. When it begins to thicken fold in the whipped cream and egg white. Turn out at once into a glass bowl and leave to set. Meanwhile peel and slice tangerines or clementines. Dissolve the redcurrant jelly over a gentle heat with about two tablespoonfuls of water to make a syrup. Strain or heat until smooth. Leave until cold. Arrange the slices of fruit over the cream and, just before serving, coat with the syrup.

Christmas pudding
ice cream

glass or metal bombe container
a little oil
4 ozs plain chocolate

8 ozs (225g) mincemeat
½ pt (300 mls) vanilla ice cream

WITH a pastry brush paint the inside of the bombe with a little oil and then turn it upside down to drain. Melt the chocolate and when runny pour it into the mould, making sure it goes into all the corners. Put into the fridge until this lining is set. Put the mincemeat into a bowl, add the ice cream and stir well together. Remove the bombe from the fridge and pour in the ice cream and mincemeat mixture. Refrigerate until an hour before ready to serve. Then dip the bombe in a bowl of very hot water for a few seconds and turn out the chocolate coated ice cream into a serving bowl or dish.

Quick party trifle

2 raspberry jam Swiss rolls, the ones
without cream
1 wine-glass medium dry sherry
1 banana, peeled and sliced

small can mandarin oranges,
drained and juice reserved
1 tin Ambrosia Devon custard
½ pt (300 mls) double cream

BREAK up the Swiss rolls into the bottom of a trifle bowl and pour over the sherry. Mix it in, squashing the sponge base well down. It should be quite wet, if not add a little more sherry or some of the juice from the tinned mandarins. Spread a layer of mandarin oranges evenly over the sponge base, then add a layer of the sliced banana. Pour the tinned custard over the bananas. Whip the cream until stiffish but spreadable. Put blobs of cream evenly all over the surface and then, with a fork or spoon, spread it over the surface to form a complete cream topping. Decorate with glace cherries and strips of angelica.

• •

CHRISTMAS GIFTS
••••••••••••••••••••

THE most acceptable of Christmas gifts are things to eat. Here are some recipes for cook-your-own presents – sweets and savouries, cheese and chutney and bottled fruit. They are not difficult or expensive to produce. The only problem is resisting the temptation to eat them all yourself.

Chocolate whisky truffles

4 ozs (100g) plain chocolate
2 ozs (50g) butter
1 tbs whisky
2 egg yolks

1 oz (25g) ground almonds
1 oz (25g) stale cake crumbs
8 ozs (225g) icing sugar, sifted
drinking chocolate to finish

BREAK up chocolate and put with the butter into a basin over a saucepan of hot water and leave to melt. Stir occasionally and then add the whiskey and egg yolks and beat well. Mix in the rest of the ingredients, except the drinking chocolate, and transfer mixture to a plate. Cool for about two hours, until firm. Roll into 36 balls, dust them in the powdered drinking chocolate and put in fluted paper cases. This recipe can be varied by using sherry or rum instead of whisky.

Cherry fudge

½ pt (300 mls) milk
1¾ lb (800g) granulated sugar
4 ozs (100g) butter

2 ozs (50g) glace cherries, chopped
2 tsp vanilla essence

BRING milk slowly to the boil in a pan and add the sugar and butter. Stir until the butter melts and sugar dissolves. Bring to the boil, cover pan and boil for two minutes. Take off the lid and continue to boil for a further 10 to 15 minutes, stirring occasionally. Test when cooked by dropping a little of the mixture in a cup of cold water. It should form a soft ball when rolled between the thumb and forefinger. If you have a sugar thermometer the temperature should be 120°C. Remove from heat, stir in the glace cherries and vanilla essence and leave to cool for five minutes. Beat fudge with a wooden spoon until it just begins to lose its gloss and is thick and creamy. Transfer to a buttered seven inch square tin and mark into squares when cool. Cut up with a sharp knife when firmly set.

Blue cheese shortbread

6 ozs (175g) plain flour
6 ozs (175g) butter
3 ozs (75g) semolina

5 ozs (150g) blue cheese, crumbled
½ tsp cayenne pepper
1 tsp salt

MIX together, with your fingers or in a food processor, the flour, salt, semolina, cayenne and the crumbled cheese. Roll out the resulting paste on a floured surface and transfer to the baking sheet. Pat down to half an inch thickness and prick all over with a fork. Cut into two inch slices and bake in a slow oven (150°C, gas 2) for 30 to 45 minutes.

Potted cheese

4 ozs (100g) blue cheese
1½ ozs (40g) butter
1 tsp sugar

pinch of mace
1 tbs white wine

POUND all the ingredients together and mix well with the wine. Form whatever shapes you like – wedges, triangles, circles – and either wrap in cling film and place in a box, or press into pots.

Apple chutney ✳

6 eating apples, peeled, cored
and quartered
4 ozs (100g) currants
4 ozs (100g) raisins
3 tomatoes, peeled and sliced
3 small onions, peeled and sliced

8 ozs (225g) light brown sugar
1 pt (600 mls) distilled vinegar
1 tbs mustard seed
1 tsp coriander
½ tbs curry powder
1 tbs salt

PUT the currants and raisins to soak in warm water for half an hour. Put the vinegar in a pan, add the sugar, curry powder, salt, cayenne and spices and stir until it comes to the boil. Add the onions, tomatoes, raisins and currants and simmer gently for 45 minutes before adding the apples and three tablespoonfuls of cold water. Bring back to the boil and simmer, giving the occasional stir, until apples are soft and the chutney is a deep golden brown. Ladle into sterilised jars and cover when cold.

Bottled apricots

apricots to fill bottle of your choice   2 ozs (50g) icing sugar per lb of fruit

BLANCH, peel and stone the fresh apricots and cut them into quarters. Leave them in a bowl overnight covered with the sifted icing sugar. Pack fruit tightly into wide necked bottles, put them into a pan of cold water and bring it to the boil. Put in the stoppers and seal securely.

Sauces

Mayonnaise

1 egg yolk
pinch of salt, pepper and mustard
4 tbs oil

1 dsp vinegar
1 dsp warm water

IF you have a liquidiser put the egg yolk, seasonings and vinegar into the container, blend them for a few seconds and then pour in the oil steadily, blending slowly as you do so, until the mixture becomes creamy. Otherwise put the egg yolk and seasonings into a bowl and gradually beat in the oil, a drop at a time, until it thickens. Too much oil and it will curdle. Beat in the vinegar gradually, followed by the warm water. Always use freshly made mayonnaise.

Quick home-made Hollandaise sauce

3 egg yolks
few drops lemon juice

1 tbs water
6 ozs butter

Put the egg-yolks into a liquidiser, add the lemon juice and water. Blend for a minute. Heat the butter until very hot and slowly pour it into the blended mixture. Remove from liquidiser to a bowl and beat with a wire whisk, adding seasoning to taste.

Hollandaise sauce
(the longer way)

1 tsp lemon juice
1 tsp wine vinegar
1 tbs cold water
3 white peppercorns

½ small bay leaf
yolks of 4 eggs
8 ozs (225g) butter, softened
salt and pepper

PUT the lemon juice, vinegar, water, bay leaf and peppercorns into a saucepan and boil gently until the liquor is reduced by half. Leave to cool, then strain into a double saucepan, on a moderate heat, and whisk in the egg yolks until the mixture is thick and foamy. Gradually add the butter, a little bit at a time and continue whisking until each piece is absorbed and the sauce takes on the consistency of mayonnaise. Season to taste and serve at once.

Tomato sauce

1½ lbs (675g) ripe tomatoes,
peeled and chopped
1 tsp olive oil
1 medium onion, peeled and
finely chopped
1 clove garlic, crushed

1 medium carrot, scraped and grated
1 tsp concentrated tomato puree
1 tbs fresh herbs (basil, tarragon
or oregano)
salt and freshly ground black pepper
4 tbs red wine

PUT olive oil in a saucepan and add the onion and garlic. Cook until softened. Add the carrot and cook for another one to two minutes then put in the tomatoes, tomato puree, herbs and seasoning. Bring to simmering point and cook for about 20 minutes until the tomatoes are completely soft. Add the wine and continue to cook for a further 10 minutes. Adjust seasoning to taste and serve hot or cold.

Caper sauce

½ oz (14g) butter
½ oz (14g) flour
½ pt (300 mls) milk

½ level tsp salt
shake of pepper
2 tbs chopped capers

MELT butter in pan, add the flour and cook over low heat, stirring all the time, for two minutes. Do not allow mixture to brown. Gradually blend in the milk. Cook, stirring constantly, until the sauce comes to the boil and thickens, then stir in the seasoning and chopped capers and simmer for a few more minutes before serving.

Bechamel sauce

½ pt (300 mls) milk
1 small onion, peeled and quartered
1 small carrot, scraped and sliced
1 stalk of celery, sliced
2 cloves
6 white peppercorns

1 blade of mace
sprig of parsley
1 oz (25g) butter
1 oz (25g) flour
2 tbs double cream
salt and pepper

PUT milk into a saucepan and add the onion, carrot, celery, peppercorns, cloves, mace and parsley. Slowly bring just to the boil then remove from the heat, cover, and leave for half an hour. Strain the milk and reserve. Melt butter in a pan. Add the flour and cook over a low heat, stirring constantly, for two minutes. Do not let it go brown. Gradually blend in the flavoured milk and cook, stirring, until the sauce comes to the boil and thickens. Simmer gently for three minutes then remove from heat and season to taste. Stir in the cream.

White sauce

1 oz (25g) butter
1 oz (25g) flour

salt and pepper
½ pt (300 mls) milk

HEAT the butter slowly, remove from heat and stir in the flour. Return to the heat and cook gently for a few minutes, taking care the mixture does not brown. Again remove from the heat and gradually add the cold milk. Bring to the boil and cook, stirring constantly with a wooden spoon, until the sauce is smooth. Season, and if there are any small lumps in the sauce, whisk it briskly to clear them.

Mustard sauce

FOLLOW the above recipe for white sauce but before seasoning with salt and pepper stir in two level teaspoonfuls of dry mustard mixed with two teaspoonfuls of vinegar.

Standard vinaigrette

3 tbs olive oil
1 tbs cider vinegar
1 tsp castor sugar

pinch of salt and ground black pepper
½ tsp made English mustard
1 clove garlic, peeled and crushed

PUT all the ingredients into a screw top jar and shake vigorously. It is a good idea to keep a jar of vinaigrette in the fridge at all times as it is needed frequently.

• •